NELSON MANDELA
I am prepared to die

Nelson Rolihlahla Mandela was born in the Transkei, South Africa, on 18 July 1918 He was educated at Fort Hare University College and the University of the Witwatersrand. He joined the African National Congress in 1944, and was elected General Secretary of the militant Youth League. In 1952 he was elected Transvaal President of the ANC and Volunteer-in-Chief of the Defiance of Unjust Laws Campaign. He was then banned from attending all gatherings and from membership of the ANC.

Mandela set up in practice as a lawyer with Oliver Tambo, now President of the ANC. On 5 December 1956, together with 154 other leading opponents of apartheid, they were both arrested and charged with high treason. The Treason Trial lasted until 29 March 1961. All the accused were acquitted, but the ANC had been outlawed after the Sharpeville massacre in 1960. In April 1961 the All-in African Conference was held in Pietermaritzburg to demand a National Convention to establish a non-racial union of all South Africans instead of the racist republic which had recently been voted for by a referendum of whites only. Mandela was elected secretary of the National Action Council which would call a general strike should the government not respond to this demand. Mandela went underground, eluding the police for 15 months, and became known as 'The Black Pimpernel'. He toured Africa and visited Britain. On 5 August 1962 he was arrested in South Africa. Extracts from the court record of his subsequent trial are on pages 1-28. He was convicted on two counts, of inciting persons to strike illegally, and of leaving the country without a valid passport, and jailed for three years.

In 1963 Mandela stood trial again, together with nine others, for sabotage in the 'Rivonia Trial'. His historic statement from the dock is on pages 28-48.

Mandela was sentenced to life imprisonment and sent to Robben Island. According to the South African government's policy on political prisoners, Mandela will be allowed no remission of sentence, amnesty or parole.

International Defence and Aid Fund for Southern Africa

Canon Collins House, 64 Essex Rd., London N1 8LR

First published 1979
Reprinted 1984

MANDELA'S 1962 TRIAL
"BLACK MAN IN A WHITE COURT"

Extracts from the court record of the trial of Mandela held in the magistrate's court in the Old Synagogue, Pretoria, from 15 October to 7 November 1962. Mandela conducted his own defence.

MANDELA: Your Worship, before I plead to the charge, there are one or two points I would like to raise.

Firstly, Your Worship will recall that this matter was postponed last Monday at my request until today, to enable Counsel to make the arrangements to be available here today. Although Counsel is now available, after consultation with him and my attorneys, I have elected to conduct my own defence. Some time during the progress of these proceedings, I hope to be able to indicate that this case is a trial of the aspirations of the African people, and because of that I thought it proper to conduct my own defence. Nevertheless, I have decided to retain the services of Counsel, who will be here throughout these proceedings, and I also would like my attorney to be available in the course of these proceedings as well, but subject to that I will conduct my own defence.

The second point I would like to raise is an application which is addressed to Your Worship. Now at the outset, I want to make it perfectly clear that the remarks I am going to make are not addressed to Your Worship in his personal capacity, nor are they intended to reflect upon the integrity of the Court. I hold Your Worship in high esteem and I do not for one single moment doubt your sense of fairness and justice. I must also mention that nothing I am going to raise in this application is intended to reflect against the Prosecutor in his personal capacity.

The point I wish to raise in my argument is based not on personal considerations, but on important questions that go beyond the scope of this present trial. I might also mention that in the course of this application I am frequently going to refer to the white man and the white people. I want at once to make it clear that I am no racialist, and I detest racialism, because I regard it as a barbaric thing, whether it comes from a black man or from a white man. The terminology that I am going to employ will be compelled on me by the nature of the application I am making.

I want to apply for Your Worship's recusal from this case. I challenge the right of this Court to hear my case on two grounds.

Firstly, I challenge it because I fear that I will not be given a fair and proper trial. Secondly, I consider myself neither legally nor morally bound to obey laws made by a Parliament in which I have no representation.

In a political trial such as this one, which involves a clash of the aspirations of the African people and those of whites, the country's courts, as presently constituted, cannot be impartial and fair.

In such cases, whites are interested parties. To have a white judicial officer presiding, however high his esteem, and however strong his sense of fairness and justice, is to make whites judges in their own case.

It is improper and against the elementary principles of justice to entrust whites with cases involving the denial by them of basic human rights to the African people.

What sort of justice is this that enables the aggrieved to sit in judgement over those against whom they have laid a charge?

A judiciary controlled entirely by whites and enforcing laws enacted by a white Parliament in which Africans have no representation—laws which in most cases are passed in the face of unanimous opposition from Africans—

MAGISTRATE: I am wondering whether I shouldn't interfere with you at this stage, Mr. Mandela. Aren't we going beyond the scope of the proceedings? After all is said and done, there is only one Court today and that is the white Man's Court. There is no other Court. What purpose does it serve you to make an application when there is only one Court, as you know yourself. What Court do you wish to be tried by?

MANDELA: Well, Your Worship, firstly I would like Your Worship to bear in mind that in a series of cases our Courts have laid it down that the right of a litigant to ask for a recusal of a judicial officer is an extremely important right, which must be given full protection by the Court, as long as that right is exercised honestly. Now I honestly have apprehensions, as I am going to demonstrate just now, that this unfair discrimination throughout my life has been responsible for very grave injustices, and I am going to contend that that race discrimination which outside this Court has been responsible for all my troubles, I fear in this Court is going to do me the same injustice. Now Your Worship may disagree with that, but Your Worship is perfectly entitled, in fact, obliged to listen to me, and because of that I feel that Your Worship—

MAGISTRATE: I would like to listen, but I would like you to give me the grounds for your application for me to recuse myself.

MANDELA: Well, these are the grounds, I am developing them, sir. If Your Worship will give me time—

MAGISTRATE: I don't wish to go out of the scope of the proceedings.

MANDELA: —Of the scope of the application. I am within the scope of the application, because I am putting forward grounds which in my opinion are likely not to give me a fair and proper trial.

MAGISTRATE: Anyway, proceed.

MANDELA: As Your Worship pleases. I was developing the point that a judiciary controlled entirely by whites and enforcing laws enacted by a white Parliament in which we have no representation, laws which in most cases are passed in the face of unanimous opposition from Africans, cannot be regarded as an impartial tribunal in a political trial where an African stands as an accused.

The Universal Declaration of Human Rights provides that all men are equal before the law, and are entitled without any discrimination to equal protection

2

of the law. In May, 1951, Dr. D. F. Malan, then Prime Minister, told the Union Parliament, that this provision of the Declaration applies in this country. Similar statements have been made on numerous occasions in the past by prominent whites in this country, including Judges and Magistrates. But the real truth is that there is in fact no equality before the law whatsoever as far as our people are concerned, and statements to the contrary are definitely incorrect and misleading.

It is true that an African who is charged in a court of law enjoys, on the surface, the same rights and privileges as an accused who is white in so far as the conduct of this trial is concerned. He is governed by the same rules of procedure and evidence as apply to a white accused. But it would be grossly inaccurate to conclude from this fact that an African consequently enjoys equality before the law.

In its proper meaning equality before the law means the right to participate in the making of the laws by which one is governed, a constitution which guarantees democratic rights to all sections of the population, the right to approach the court for protection or relief in the case of the violation of rights guaranteed in the constitution, and the right to take part in the administration of justice as judges, magistrates, attorneys-general, law advisers and similar positions.

In the absence of these safeguards the phrase 'equality before the law', in so far as it is intended to apply to us, is meaningless and misleading. All the rights and privileges to which I have referred are monopolized by whites, and we enjoy none of them.

The white man makes all the laws, he drags us before his courts and accuses us, and he sits in judgement over us.

It is fit and proper to raise the question sharply, what is this rigid colour-bar in the administration of justice? Why is it that in this courtroom I face a white magistrate, am confronted by a white prosecutor, and escorted into the dock by a white orderly? Can anyone honestly and seriously suggest that in this type of atmosphere the scales of justice are evenly balanced?

Why is it that no African in the history of this country has ever had the honour of being tried by his own kith and kin, by his own flesh and blood?

I will tell Your Worship why: the real purpose of this rigid colour-bar is to ensure that the justice dispensed by the courts should conform to the policy of the country, however much that policy might be in conflict with the norms of justice accepted in judiciaries throughout the civilized world.

I feel oppressed by the atmosphere of white domination that lurks all around in this courtroom. Somehow this atmosphere calls to mind the inhuman injustices caused to my people outside this courtroom by this same white domination.

It reminds me that I am voteless because there is a Parliament in this country that is white-controlled. I am without land because the white minority has taken a lion's share of my country and forced me to occupy poverty-stricken

Reserves, over-populated and over-stocked. We are ravaged by starvation and disease. . . .

MAGISTRATE: What has that got to do with the case, Mr. Mandela?

MANDELA: With the last point, Sir, it hangs together, if Your Worship will give me the chance to develop it.

MAGISTRATE: You have been developing for quite a while now, and I feel you are going beyond the scope of your application.

MANDELA: Your Worship, this to me is an extremely important ground which the Court must consider.

MAGISTRATE: I fully realise your position, Mr. Mandela, but you must confine yourself to the application and not go beyond it. I don't want to know about starvation. That in my view has got nothing to do with the case at the present moment.

MANDELA: Well, Your Worship has already raised the point that here in this country there is only a white Court. What is the point of all this? Now if I can demonstrate to Your Worship that outside this Courtroom race discrimination has been used in such a way as to deprive me of my rights, not to treat me fairly, certainly this is a relevant fact from which to infer that wherever race discrimination is practised, this will be the same result, and this is the only reason why I am using this point.

MAGISTRATE: I am afraid that I will have to interrupt you, and you will have to confine yourself to the reasons, the real reasons for asking me to recuse myself.

MANDELA: Your Worship, the next point which I want to make is this: I raise the question, how can I be expected to believe that this same racial discrimination which has been the cause of so much injustice and suffering right through the years should now operate here to give me a fair and open trial? Is there no danger that an African accused may regard the courts not as impartial tribunals, dispensing justice without fear or favour, but as instruments used by the white man to punish those amongst us who clamour for deliverance from the fiery furnace of white rule. I have grave fears that this system of justice may enable the guilty to drag the innocent before the courts. It enables the unjust to prosecute and demand vengeance against the just. It may tend to lower the standards of fairness and justice applied in the country's courts by white judicial officers to black litigants. This is the first ground for this application: that I will not receive a fair and proper trial.

The second ground of my objection is that I consider myself neither morally nor legally obliged to obey laws made by a Parliament in which I am not represented.

That the will of the people is the basis of the authority of government is a principle universally acknowledged as sacred throughout the civilized world, and constitutes the basic foundations of freedom and justice. It is understandable why citizens, who have the vote as well as the right to direct representation in the country's governing bodies, should be morally and legally bound by the laws governing the country.

It should be equally understandable why we, as Africans, should adopt the attitude that we are neither morally nor legally bound to obey laws which we have not made, nor can we be expected to have confidence in courts which enforce such laws.

I am aware that in many cases of this nature in the past, South African courts have upheld the right of the African people to work for democratic changes. Some of our judicial officers have even openly criticized the policy which refuses to acknowledge that all men are born free and equal, and fearlessly condemned the denial of opportunities to our people.

But such exceptions exist in spite of, not because of, the grotesque system of justice that has been built up in this country. These exceptions furnish yet another proof that even among the country's whites there are honest men whose sense of fairness and justice revolts against the cruelty perpetrated by their own white brothers to our people.

The existence of genuine democratic values among some of the country's whites in the judiciary, however slender they may be, is welcomed by me. But I have no illusions about the significance of this fact, healthy a sign as it might be. Such honest and upright whites are few and they have certainly not succeeded in convincing the vast majority of the rest of the white population that white supremacy leads to dangers and disaster.

However, it would be a hopeless commandant who relied for his victories on the few soldiers in the enemy camp who sympathize with his cause. A competent general pins his faith on the superior striking power he commands and on the justness of his cause which he must pursue uncompromisingly to the bitter end.

I hate race discrimination most intensely and in all its manifestations. I have fought it all during my life; I fight it now, and will do so until the end of my days. Even although I now happen to be tried by one whose opinion I hold in high esteem, I detest most violently the set-up that surrounds me here. It makes me feel that I am a black man in a white man's court. This should not be. I should feel perfectly at ease and at home with the assurance that I am being tried by a fellow South African who does not regard me as an inferior, entitled to a special type of justice.

This is not the type of atmosphere most conducive to feelings of security and confidence in the impartiality of a court.

The Court might reply to this part of my argument by assuring me that it will try my case fairly and without fear or favour, that in deciding whether or not I am guilty of the offence charged by the State, the Court will not be influenced by the colour of my skin or by any other improper motive.

That might well be so. But such a reply would completely miss the point of my argument.

5

As already indicated, my objection is not directed to Your Worship in his personal capacity, nor is it intended to reflect upon the integrity of the Court. My objection is based upon the fact that our courts, as presently constituted, create grave doubts in the minds of an African accused, whether he will receive a fair and proper trial.

This doubt springs from objective facts relating to the practice of unfair discrimination against the black man in the constitution of the country's courts. Such doubts cannot be allayed by mere verbal assurances from a presiding officer, however sincere such assurances might be. There is only one way, and one way only, of allaying such doubts, namely, by removing unfair discrimination in judicial appointments. This is my first difficulty.

I have yet another difficulty about similar assurances Your Worship might give. Broadly speaking, Africans and whites in this country have no common standard of fairness, morality, and ethics, and it would be very difficult to determine on my part what standard of fairness and justice Your Worship has in mind.

In their relationship with us, South African whites regard it as fair and just to pursue policies which have outraged the conscience of mankind and of honest and upright men throughout the civilized world. They suppress our aspirations, bar our way to freedom, and deny us opportunities to promote our moral and material progress, to secure ourselves from fear and want. All the good things of life are reserved for the white folk and we blacks are expected to be content to nourish our bodies with such pieces of food as drop from the tables of men with white skins. This is the white man's standard of justice and fairness. Herein lies his conception of ethics. Whatever he himself may say in his defence, the white man's moral standards in this country must be judged by the extent to which he has condemned the vast majority of its inhabitants to serfdom and inferiority.

We, on the other hand, regard the struggle against colour discrimination and for the pursuit of freedom and happiness as the highest aspiration of all men. Through bitter experience, we have learnt to regard the white man as a harsh and merciless type of human being whose contempt for our rights, and whose utter indifference to the promotion of our welfare, makes his assurances to us absolutely meaningless and hypocritical.

I have the hope and confidence that Your Worship will not hear this objection lightly nor regard it as frivolous. I have decided to speak frankly and honestly because the injustice I have referred to contains the seeds of an extremely dangerous situation for our country and people. I make no threat when I say that unless these wrongs are remedied without delay, we might well find that even plain talk before the country's courts is too timid a method to draw the attention of the country to our political demands.

Finally, I need only say that the courts have said that the possibility of bias and not actual bias is all that need be proved to ground an application of this nature. In this application I have merely referred to certain objective facts, from which I submit that the possibility be inferred that I will not receive a fair and proper trial.

MAGISTRATE: Mr. Prosecutor, have you anything to say?

PROSECUTOR: Very briefly, Your Worship, I just wish to point out that there are certain legal grounds upon which an accused person is entitled to apply for the recusal of a judicial officer from the case in which he is to be tried. I submit that the Accused's application is not based on one of those principles, and I ask the Court to reject it.

MAGISTRATE: [*to Mandela*] Your application is dismissed. Will you now plead to your charges?

MANDELA: I plead NOT GUILTY to both charges, to all the charges.

Among the witnesses was Mr. Barnard, the private secretary to the then Prime Minister, Dr. H. F. Verwoerd, whom Mandela cross-examined on the subject of a letter sent by Mandela to the Prime Minister demanding a National Convention in May 1961. In cross-examining the witness, Mandela first read the contents of the letter:

"I am directed by the All-In African National Action Council to address your Government in the following terms:

The All-In African National Action Council was established in terms of a resolution adopted at a conference held at Pietermaritzburg on 25 and 26 March 1961. This conference was attended by 1,500 delegates from town and country, representing 145 religious, social, cultural, sporting, and political bodies.

Conference noted that your Government, after receiving a mandate from a section of the European population, decided to proclaim a Republic on 31 May.

It was the firm view of delegates that your Government, which represents only a minority of the population in this country, is not entitled to take such a decision without first seeking the views and obtaining the express consent of the African people. Conference feared that under this proposed Republic your Government, which is already notorious the world over for its obnoxious policies, would continue to make even more savage attacks on the rights and living conditions of the African people.

Conference carefully considered the grave political situation facing the African people today. Delegate after delegate drew attention to the vicious manner in which your Government forced the people of Zeerust, Sekhukhuniland, Pondoland, Nongoma, Tembuland and other areas to accept the unpopular system of Bantu Authorities, and pointed to numerous facts and incidents which indicate the rapid manner in which race relations are deteriorating in this country.

It was the earnest opinion of Conference that this dangerous situation could be averted only by the calling of a sovereign national convention representative of all South Africans, to draw up a new non-racial and democratic Constitution. Such a convention would discuss our national problems in a sane and sober manner, and would work out solutions which sought to preserve and safeguard the interests of all sections of the population.

Conference unanimously decided to call upon your Government to summon such a convention before 31 May.

Conference further decided that unless your Government calls the convention before the above-mentioned date, country-wide demonstrations would be held on the eve of the Republic in protest. Conference also resolved that in addition to the demonstrations, the African people would be called upon to refuse to co-operate with the proposed Republic.

We attach the Resolutions of the Conference for your attention and necessary action.

We now demand that your Government call the convention before 31 May, failing which we propose to adopt the steps indicated in paragraphs 8 and 9 of this letter.

These demonstrations will be conducted in a disciplined and peaceful manner.

We are fully aware of the implications of this decision, and the action we propose taking. We have no illusions about the counter-measures your Government might take in this matter. After all, South Africa and the world know that during the last thirteen years your Government has subjected us to merciless and arbitrary rule. Hundreds of our people have been banned and confined to certain areas. Scores have been banished to remote parts of the country, and many arrested and jailed for a multitude of offences. It has become extremely difficult to hold meetings, and freedom of speech has been drastically curtailed. During the last twelve months we have gone through a period of grim dictatorship, during which seventy-five people were killed and hundreds injured while peacefully demonstrating against passes.

Political organizations were declared unlawful, and thousands flung into jail without trial. Your Government can only take these measures to suppress the forthcoming demonstrations, and these measures have failed to stop opposition to the policies of your Government. We are not deterred by threats of force and violence made by you and your Government, and will carry out our duty without flinching."

MANDELA: You remember the contents of this letter?

WITNESS: I do.

MANDELA: Did you place this letter before your Prime Minister?

WITNESS: Yes.

MANDELA: On what date? Can you remember?

WITNESS: It is difficult to remember, but I gather from the date specified on the date stamp, the Prime Minister's Office date stamp.

MANDELA: That is 24 April. Now was any reply given to this letter by the Prime Minister? Did he reply to this letter?

WITNESS: He did not reply to the writer.

MANDELA: He did not reply to the letter. Now, will you agree that this letter raises matters of vital concern to the vast majority of the citizens of this country?

WITNESS: I do not agree.

MANDELA: You don't agree? You don't agree that the question of human rights, of civil liberties, is a matter of vital importance to the African people?

WITNESS: Yes, that is so, indeed.

MANDELA: Are these things mentioned here?

WITNESS: Yes, I think so.

MANDELA: They are mentioned. You agree that this letter deals with matters of vital importance to the African people in this country? You have already agreed that this letter raises questions like the rights of freedom, civil liberties, and so on?

WITNESS: Yes, the letter raises it.

MANDELA: Important questions to any citizen?

WITNESS: Yes.

MANDELA: Now, you know of course that Africans don't enjoy the rights demanded in this letter. They are denied the rights of government?

WITNESS: Some rights.

MANDELA: No African is a Member of Parliament?

WITNESS: That is right.

MANDELA: No African can be a Member of the Provincial Council, of the Municipal Councils?

WITNESS: Yes.

MANDELA: Africans have no vote in this country?

WITNESS: They have got no vote as far as Parliament is concerned.

MANDELA: Yes, that is what I am talking about, I am talking about Parliament, and other government bodies of the country, the Provincial Councils, the Municipal Councils. They have no vote?

WITNESS: That is right.

MANDELA: Would you agree with me that in any civilized country in the world it would be at least most scandalous for a Prime Minister to fail to reply to a letter raising vital issues affecting the majority of the citizens of that country. Would you agree with that?

WITNESS: I don't agree with that.

MANDELA: You don't agree that it would be irregular for a Prime Minister to ignore a letter raising vital issues affecting the vast majority of the citizens of that country?

WITNESS: This letter has not been ignored by the Prime Minister.

MANDELA: Just answer the question. Do you regard it proper for a Prime Minister not to respond to pleas made in regard to vital issues by the vast majority of the citizens of the country? You say that is not wrong?

WITNESS: The Prime Minister did respond to the letter.

9

MANDELA: Mr. Barnard, I don't want to be rude to you. Will you confine yourself to answering my questions? The question I am putting to you is, do you agree that it is most improper on the part of a Prime Minister not to reply to a communication raising vital issues affecting the vast majority of the country?

WITNESS: I do not agree in this special case, because . . .

MANDELA: As a general proposition? Would you regard it as improper, speaking generally, for a Prime Minister not to respond to a letter of this nature, that is a letter raising vital issues affecting the majority of the citizens?

PROSECUTOR: (*Intervened with objections to the line of questioning*)

MANDELA: You say that the Prime Minister did not ignore this letter?

WITNESS: He did not acknowledge the letter to the writer.

MANDELA: This letter was not ignored by the Prime Minister?

WITNESS: No, it was not ignored.

MANDELA: It was attended to?

WITNESS: It was indeed.

MANDELA: In what way?

WITNESS: According to the usual procedure, and that is that the Prime Minister refers correspondence to the respective Minister, the Minister most responsible for that particular letter.

MANDELA: Was this letter referred to another Department?

WITNESS: That is right.

MANDELA: Which Department?

WITNESS: The Department of Justice.

MANDELA: Can you explain why I was not favoured with the courtesy of an acknowledgement of this letter, and also the explanation that it had been referred to the appropriate Department for attention?

WITNESS: When a letter is replied to and whether it should be replied to, depends on the contents of the letter in many instances.

MANDELA: My question is, can you explain to me why I was not favoured with the courtesy of an acknowledgement of the letter, irrespective of what the Prime Minister is going to do about it? Why was I not favoured with this courtesy?

WITNESS: Because of the contents of this letter.

MANDELA: Because it raises vital issues?

WITNESS: Because of the contents of the letter.

MANDELA: I see. This is not the type of thing the Prime Minister would ever consider responding to?

WITNESS: The Prime Minister did respond.

MANDELA: You say that the issues raised in this letter are not the type of thing your Prime Minister could ever respond to?

WITNESS: The whole tone of the letter was taken into consideration.

MANDELA: The tone of the letter demanding a National Convention? Of all South Africans? That is the tone of the letter? That is not the type of thing your Prime Minister could ever respond to?

WITNESS: The tone of the letter indicates whether, and to what extent, the Prime Minister responds to correspondence.

MANDELA: I want to put it to you that in failing to respond to this letter, your Prime Minister fell below the standards which one expects from one in such a position.

Now this letter, Exhibit 18, is dated 26 June 1961, and it is also addressed to the Prime Minister, and it reads as follows:

"I refer you to my letter of 20 April 1961, to which you do not have the courtesy to reply or acknowledge receipt. In the letter referred to above I informed you of the resolutions passed by the All-In African National Conference in Pietermaritzburg on 26 March 1961, demanding the calling by your Government before 31 May 1961 of a multi-racial and sovereign National Convention to draw up a new non-racial and democratic Constitution for South Africa. The Conference Resolution which was attached to my letter indicated that if your Government did not call this Convention by the specific date, country-wide demonstrations would be staged to mark our protest against the White Republic forcibly imposed on us by a minority. The Resolution further indicated that in addition to the demonstrations, the African people would be called upon not to co-operate with the Republican Government, or with any Government based on force. As your Government did not respond to our demands, the All-In African National Council, which was entrusted by the Conference with the task of implementing its resolutions, called for a General Strike on the 29th, 30th, and 31st of last month. As predicted in my letter of 30 April 1961, your Government sought to suppress the strike by force. You rushed a special law in Parliament authorizing the detention without trial of people connected with the organization of the strike. The army was mobilized and European civilians armed. More than ten thousand innocent Africans were arrested under the pass laws and meetings banned throughout the country. Long before the factory gates were opened on Monday, 29 May 1961, senior police officers and Nationalist South Africans spread a deliberate falsehood and announced that the strike had failed. All these measures failed to break the strike and our people stood up magnificently and gave us solid and substantial support. Factory and office workers, businessmen in town and country, students in university colleges, in the primary and secondary schools, rose to the occasion and recorded in clear terms their opposition to the Republic. The Government is guilty of self-deception if they say that non-Europeans did not respond to the call. Considerations of honesty demand of your Government to realize that the African people who constitute four-fifths of the country's population are against your Republic. As indicated above, the Pietermaritzburg resolution provided that in addition to the country-wide demonstrations, the African people would refuse to cooperate with the Republic or any form of government based on force. Failure by your Government to call the Convention makes it imperative for us to launch a full-scale and country-wide campaign for non-co-operation with your Government. There are two alternatives before you. Either you accede to our demands and call a National Convention of all South Africans to draw up a democratic Constitution, which will end the frightful policies of racial oppression pursued by your Government. By pursuing this course and abandoning the repressive and dangerous policies of your Government, you may still save our country from economic dislocation and ruin and from civil strife and bitterness. Alternatively, you may choose to persist with the present policies which are cruel and dishonest and which are opposed by millions of people here and abroad. For our own part, we wish to make it perfectly clear that we shall never cease to fight against repression and injustice, and we are resuming active opposition against your régime. In taking this decision we must again stress that we have no illusions of the serious implications of our decision. We know that your Government will once again unleash all its fury and barbarity to persecute the African people. But as the result of the last strike has clearly proved, no power on earth can stop an oppressed people, determined to win their freedom. History punishes those who resort to force and fraud to suppress the claims and legitimate aspirations of the majority of the country's citizens."

MANDELA: This is the letter which you received on 28 June 1961? Again there was no acknowledgement or reply by the Prime Minister to this letter?

WITNESS: I don't think it is—I think it shouldn't be called a letter in the first instance, but an accumulation of threats.

MANDELA: Whatever it is, there was no reply to it?

WITNESS: No.

Another witness to be called was Warrant Officer Baardman, member of the police Special Branch in Bloemfontein. He was cross-examined by Mandela:

MANDELA: Is it true to say that the present constitution of South Africa was passed at a National Convention representing whites only?

WITNESS: I don't know, I was not there.

MANDELA: But from your knowledge?

WITNESS: I don't know, I was not there.

MANDELA: You don't know at all?

WITNESS: No, I don't know.

MANDELA: You want this Court to believe that, that you don't know?

WITNESS: I don't know, I was not there.

MANDELA: Just let me put the question. You don't know that the National Convention in 1909 was a convention of whites only?

WITNESS: I don't know, I was not there.

MANDELA: Do you know that the Union Parliament is an all-White Parliament?

WITNESS: Yes, with representation for non-Whites.

MANDELA: Now, I just want to ask you one or two personal questions. What standard of education have you passed?

WITNESS: Matriculation.

MANDELA: When was that?

WITNESS: In 1932.

MANDELA: In what medium did you write it?

WITNESS: In my mother tongue. (*Here the witness meant Afrikaans.*)

MANDELA: I notice you are very proud of this?

WITNESS: I am.

MANDELA: You know of course that in this country we have no language rights as Africans?

WITNESS: I don't agree with you.

MANDELA: None of our languages is an official language, for example. Would you agree with that?

WITNESS: They are perhaps not in the Statute Book as official languages, but no one forbids you from using your own language.

MANDELA: Will you answer the question? Is it true that in this country there are only two official languages, and they are English and Afrikaans?

WITNESS: I agree entirely. By name they are the two official languages, but no one has ever forbidden you to use your own language.

MANDELA: Is it true that there are only two official languages in this country, that is English and Afrikaans?

WITNESS: To please you, that is so.

MANDELA: Is it true that the Afrikaner people in this country have fought for equality of English and Afrikaans? There was a time, for example, when Afrikaans was not the official language in the history of the various colonies, like the Cape?

WITNESS: Yes, I agree with you entirely. Constitutionally, the Afrikaner did fight for his language but not through agitators.

On the third day of the trial Mandela again applied for the recusal of the magistrate.

MANDELA: I want to make application for the recusal of Your Worship from this case. As I indicated last Monday, I hold Your Worship in high esteem, and I do not for one single moment doubt Your Worship's sense of fairness and justice. I still do, as I assured Your Worship last Monday. I make this application with the greatest of respect. I have been placed in possession of information to the effect that after the adjournment yesterday, Your

13

Worship was seen leaving the Courtroom in the company of Warrant Officer Dirker of the Special Branch, and another member of the Special Branch. As Your Worship will remember, Warrant Officer Dirker gave evidence in this case on the first day of the trial. The State Prosecutor then indicated that he would be called later, on another aspect of this case. I was then given permission by the Court to defer my cross-examination of this witness until then. The second member of the Special Branch who was in the company of Your Worship, has been seen throughout this trial assisting the State Prosecutor in presenting the case against me. Your Worship was seen entering a small blue Volkswagen car; it is believed that Your Worship sat in front, as Warrant Officer Dirker drove the car. And this other member of the Special Branch sat behind. At about ten to two Your Worship was seen returning with Warrant Officer Dirker and this other member of the Special Branch.

Now, it is not known what communication passed between Your Worship and Warrant Officer Dirker and this other member of the Special Branch. I, as an accused, was not there, and was not represented. Now, these facts have created an impression in my mind that the Court has associated itself with the State case. I am left with the substantial fear that justice is being administered in a secret manner. It is an elementary rule of justice that a judicial officer should not communicate or associate in any manner whatsoever with a party to those proceedings. I submit that Your Worship should not have acted in this fashion, and I must therefore ask Your Worship to recuse yourself from this case.

MAGISTRATE: I can only say this, that it is not for me here to give you any reasons. I can assure you, as I here now do, that I did not communicate with these two gentlemen, and your application is refused.

Another police witness was Mr. A. Moolla, an Indian member of the Special Branch, who was also cross-examined by Mandela:

MANDELA: You know about the Group Areas Act?

WITNESS: I do.

MANDELA: You know that it is intended to set certain areas for occupation by the various population groups in the country?

WITNESS: Yes, I do know.

MANDELA: And you know that it has aroused a great deal of feeling and opposition from the Indian community in this country?

WITNESS: Well, not that I know of. I think that most of the Indians are satisfied with it.

MANDELA: Is this a sincere opinion?

WITNESS: That is my sincere opinion, from people that I have met.

MANDELA: And are you aware of the attitude of the South African Indian Congress, about the Group Areas?

WITNESS: Yes.

MANDELA: What is the attitude of the South African Indian Congress?

WITNESS: The South African Indian Congress is against it.

MANDELA: And the attitude of the Transvaal Indian Congress?

WITNESS: Also.

MANDELA: They are against it?

WITNESS: Yes.

MANDELA: And the Transvaal Indian Youth Congress?

WITNESS: Also.

MANDELA: The Cape Indian Assembly, also against it?

WITNESS: Yes. Well, the Cape Indian Assembly I do not know about.

MANDELA: Well, you can take it from me that it is against it. Now, of course, if the Group Areas Act is carried out in its present form, it means that a large number of Indian merchants would lose their trading rights in areas which have been declared White Areas?

WITNESS: That is right.

MANDELA: And a large number of members of the Indian community who are living at the present moment in areas which might or have been declared as White Areas, would have to leave those homes, and have to go where they are to be stationed?

WITNESS: I think they will be better off than where ...

MANDELA: Answer the question. You know that?

WITNESS: Yes, I know that.

MANDELA: You say that the Indian merchant class in this country, who are going to lose their business rights, are happy about it?

WITNESS: Well, not all.

MANDELA: Not all. And you are saying that those members of the Indian community who are going to be driven away from the areas where they are living at present would be happy to do so?

WITNESS: Yes they would be.

MANDELA: Well, Mr. Moolla, I want to leave it at that, but just to say that you have lost your soul.

Following the closure of the prosecution case against him, Mandela addressed the Court:

I am charged with inciting people to commit an offence by way of protest against the law, a law which neither I nor any of my people had any say in preparing. The law against which the protest was directed is the law which established a Republic in the Union of South Africa. I am also charged with leaving the country without a passport. This Court has found that I am guilty of incitement to commit an offence in opposition to this law as well as of leaving the country. But in weighing up the decision as to the sentence which is to be imposed for such an offence, the Court must take into account the question of responsibility, whether it is I who is responsible or whether, in fact, a large measure of the responsibility does not lie on the shoulders of the Government which promulgated that law, knowing that my people, who constitute the majority of the population of this country, were opposed to that law, and knowing further that every legal means of demonstrating that opposition had been closed to them by prior legislation, and by Government administrative action.

The starting point in the case against me is the holding of the conference in Pietermaritzburg on 25 and 26 March last year [1961], known as the All-In African Conference, which was called by a committee which had been established by leading people and spokesmen of the whole African population, to consider the situation which was being created by the promulgation of the Republic in the country, without consultation with us, and without our consent. That conference unanimously rejected the decision of the Government, acting only in the name of and with the agreement of the white minority of this country, to establish a Republic.

It is common knowledge that the conference decided that, in place of the unilateral proclamation of a Republic by the White minority of South Africans only, it would demand in the name of the African people the calling of a truly national convention representative of all South Africans, irrespective of their colour, black and white, to sit amicably round a table, to debate a new constitution for South Africa, which was in essence what the Government was doing by the proclamation of a Republic, and furthermore, to press on behalf of the African people, that such new constitution should differ from the constitution of the proposed South African Republic by guaranteeing democratic rights on a basis of full equality to all South Africans of adult age. The conference had assembled, knowing full well that for a long period the present National Party Government of the Union of South Africa had refused to deal with, to discuss with, or to take into consideration the views of, the overwhelming majority of the South African population on this question. And, therefore, it was not enough for this conference just to proclaim its aim, but it was also necessary for the conference to find a means of stating that aim strongly and powerfully, despite the Government's unwillingness to listen.

Accordingly it was decided that should the Government fail to summon such a National Convention before 31 May 1961, all sections of the population would be called on to stage a general strike for a period of three days, both to mark our protest against the establishment of a Republic, based completely on white domination over a non-white majority, and also, in a last attempt to persuade the Government to heed our legitimate claims, and thus to avoid a period of increasing bitterness and hostility and discord in South Africa.

At that conference, an Action Council was elected, and I became its secretary. It was my duty, as secretary of the committee, to establish the machinery necessary for publicizing the decision of this conference and for directing the campaign of propaganda, publicity, and organization which would flow from it.

16

The Court is aware of the fact that I am an attorney by profession and no doubt the question will be asked why I, as an attorney who is bound, as part of my code of behaviour, to observe the laws of the country and to respect its customs and traditions, should willingly lend myself to a campaign whose ultimate aim was to bring about a strike against the proclaimed policy of the Government of this country.

In order that the Court shall understand the frame of mind which leads me to action such as this, it is necessary for me to explain the background to my own political development and to try to make this Court aware of the factors which influenced me in deciding to act as I did.

Many years ago, when I was a boy brought up in my village in the Transkei, I listened to the elders of the tribe telling stories about the good old days, before the arrival of the white man. Then our people lived peacefully, under the democratic rule of their kings and their 'amapakati', and moved freely and confidently up and down the country without let or hindrance. Then the country was ours, in our own name and right. We occupied the land, the forests, the rivers; we extracted the mineral wealth beneath the soil and all the riches of this beautiful country. We set up and operated our own Government, we controlled our own armies and we organized our own trade and commerce. The elders would tell tales of the wars fought by our ancestors in defence of the fatherland, as well as the acts of valour performed by generals and soldiers during those epic days. The names of Dingane and Bambata, among the Zulus, of Hintsa, Makana, Ndlambe of the Amaxhosa, of Sekhukhuni and others in the north, were mentioned as the pride and glory of the entire African nation.

I hoped and vowed then that, among the treasures that life might offer me, would be the opportunity to serve my people and make my own humble contribution to their freedom struggles.

The structure and organization of early African societies in this country fascinated me very much and greatly influenced the evolution of my political outlook. The land, then the main means of production, belonged to the whole tribe, and there was no individual ownership whatsoever. There were no classes, no rich or poor and no exploitation of man by man. All men were free and equal and this was the foundation of government. Recognition of this general principle found expression in the constitution of the council, variously called Imbizo, or Pitso, or Kgotla, which governs the affairs of the tribe. The council was so completely democratic that all members of the tribe could participate in its deliberations. Chief and subject, warrior and medicine man, all took part and endeavoured to influence its decisions. It was so weighty and influential a body that no step of any importance could ever be taken by the tribe without reference to it.

There was much in such a society that was primitive and insecure and it certainly could never measure up to the demands of the present epoch. But in such a society are contained the seeds of revolutionary democracy in which none will be held in slavery or servitude, and in which poverty, want, and insecurity shall be no more. This is the inspiration which, even today, inspires me and my colleagues in our political struggle.

When I reached adult stature, I became a member of the African National Congress. That was in 1944 and I have followed its policy, supported it, and believed in its aims and outlook for eighteen years. Its policy was one which appealed to my deepest inner convictions. It sought for the unity of all Africans, overriding tribal differences among them. It sought the acquisition of political power for Africans in the land of their birth. The African National Congress further believed that all people, irrespective of the national groups to which they may belong, and irrespective of the colour of their skins, all people whose home is South Africa and who believe in the principles of democracy and of equality of men, should be treated as Africans; that all South Africans are entitled to live a free life on the basis of fullest equality of the rights and opportunities in every field, of full democratic rights, with a direct say in the affairs of the Government.

These principles have been embodied in the Freedom Charter, which none in this country will dare challenge for its place as the most democratic programme of political principles ever enunciated by any political party or organization in this country. It was for me a matter of joy and pride to be a member of an organization which has proclaimed so democratic a policy and which campaigned for it militantly and fearlessly. The principles enumerated in the Charter have not been those of African people alone, for whom the African National Congress has always been the spokesman. Those principles have been adopted as well by the Indian people and the South African Indian Congress; by a section of the Coloured people, through the South African Coloured People's Congress, and also by a farsighted, forward-looking section of the European population, whose organization in days gone by was the South African Congress of Democrats. All these organizations, like the African National Congress, supported completely the demand for one man, one vote.

Right at the beginning of my career as an attorney I encountered difficulties imposed on me because of the colour of my skin, and further difficulty surrounding me because of my membership and support of the African National Congress. I discovered, for example, that unlike a white attorney, I could not occupy business premises in the city unless I first obtained ministerial consent in terms of the Urban Areas Act. I applied for that consent, but it was never granted. Although I subsequently obtained a permit, for a limited period, in terms of the Group Areas Act, that soon expired, and the authorities refused to renew it. They insisted that my partner, Oliver Tambo, and I should leave the city and practise in an African location at the back of beyond, miles away from where clients could reach us during working hours. This was tantamount to asking us to abandon our legal practice, to give up the legal service of our people, for which we had spent many years training. No attorney worth his salt will agree easily to do so. For some years, therefore, we continued to occupy premises in the city, illegally. The threat of prosecution and ejection hung menacingly over us throughout that period. It was an act of defiance of the law. We were aware that it was, but, nevertheless, that act had been forced on us against our wishes, and we could do no other than to choose between compliance with the law and compliance with our consciences.

In the courts where we practised we were treated courteously by many officials but we were very often discriminated against by some and treated with resentment and hostility by others. We were constantly aware that no matter how well, how correctly, how adequately we pursued our career of law, we could not become a prosecutor, or a magistrate, or a judge. We became aware of the fact that as attorneys we often dealt with officials whose competence and attainments were no higher than ours, but whose superior position was maintained and protected by a white skin.

I regarded it as a duty which I owed, not just to my people, but also to my profession, to the practice of law, and to justice for all mankind, to cry out against this discrimination which is essentially unjust and opposed to the whole basis of the attitude towards justice which is part of the tradition of legal training in this country. I believed that in taking up a stand against this injustice I was upholding the dignity of what should be an honourable profession.

Nine years ago the Transvaal Law Society applied to the Supreme Court to have my name struck off the roll because of the part I had played in a campaign initiated by the African National Congress, a campaign for the Defiance of Unjust Laws. During the campaign more than 8,000 of the most advanced and farseeing of my people deliberately courted arrest and imprisonment by breaking specified laws, which we regarded then, as we still do now, as unjust and repressive. In the opinion of the Law Society, my activity in connection with that campaign did not conform to the standards of conduct expected from members of our honourable profession, but on this occasion the Supreme Court held that I had been within my rights as an attorney, that there was nothing dishonourable in an attorney identifying himself with his people in their struggle for political rights, even if his activities should infringe upon the laws of the country; the Supreme Court rejected the application of the Law Society.

It would not be expected that with such a verdict in my favour I should discontinue my political activities. But Your Worship may well wonder why it is that I should find it necessary to persist with such conduct, which has not only brought me the difficulties I have referred to, but which has resulted in my spending some four years on a charge before the courts, of high treason, of which I was subsequently acquitted, and of many months in jail on no charge at all, merely on the basis of the Government's dislike of my views and of my activities during the whole period of the Emergency of 1960.

Your Worship, I would say that the whole life of any thinking African in this country drives him continuously to a conflict between his conscience on the one hand and the law on the other. This is not a conflict peculiar to this country. The conflict arises for men of conscience, for men who think and who feel deeply in every country. Recently in Britain, a peer of the realm, Earl

19

Russell, probably the most respected philosopher of the Western world, was sentenced, convicted for precisely the type of activities for which I stand before you today, for following his conscience in defiance of the law, as a protest against a nuclear weapons policy being followed by his own Government. For him, his duty to the public, his belief in the morality of the essential rightness of the cause for which he stood, rose superior to this high respect for the law. He could not do other than to oppose the law and to suffer the consequences for it. Nor can I. Nor can many Africans in this country. The law as it is applied, the law as it has been developed over a long period of history, and especially the law as it is written and designed by the Nationalist Government, is a law which, in our view, is immoral, unjust, and intolerable. Our consciences dictate that we must protest against it, that we must oppose it, and that we must attempt to alter it.

Always we have been conscious of our obligations as citizens to avoid breaches of the law, where such breaches can be avoided, to prevent a clash between the authorities and our people, where such clash can be prevented, but nevertheless, we have been driven to speak up for what we believe is right, and to work for it and to try and bring about changes which will satisfy our human conscience.

Throughout its fifty years of existence the African National Congress, for instance, has done everything possible to bring its demands to the attention of successive South African Governments. It has sought at all times peaceful solutions for all the country's ills and problems. The history of the ANC is filled with instances where deputations were sent to South African Governments either on specific issues or on the general political demands of our people. I do not wish to burden Your Worship by enunciating the occasions when such deputations were sent; all that I wish to indicate at this stage is that, in addition to the efforts made by former presidents of the ANC, when Mr. Strijdom became Prime Minister of this country, my leader, Chief A. J. Lutuli, then President of our organization, made yet another effort to persuade this Government to consider and to heed our point of view. In his letter to the Prime Minister at the time, Chief Lutuli exhaustively reviewed the country's relations and its dangers, and expressed the view that a meeting between the Government and African leaders had become necessary and urgent.

This statesmanlike and correct behaviour on the part of the leader of the majority of the South African population did not find an appropriate answer from the leader of the South African Government. The standard of behaviour of the South African Government towards my people, and its aspirations has not always been what it should have been, and is not always the standard which is to be expected in serious high-level dealings between civilized peoples. Chief Lutuli's letter was not even favoured with the courtesy of an acknowledgement from the Prime Minister's office.

This experience was repeated after the Pietermaritzburg conference, when I, as Secretary of the Action Council, elected at that conference, addressed a letter to the Prime Minister, Dr. Verwoerd, informing him of the resolution which had been taken, and calling on him to initiate steps for the convening of such a national convention as we suggested, before the date specified in the resolution. In a civilized country one would be outraged by the failure of the head of Government even to acknowledge receipt of a letter, or to consider such a reasonable request put to him by a broadly representative collection of important personalities and leaders of the most important community of the country. Once again, Government standards in dealing with my people fell below what the civilized world would expect. No reply, no response whatsoever, was received to our letter, no indication was even given that it had received any consideration whatsoever. Here we, the African people, and especially we of the National Action Council, who had been entrusted with the tremendous responsibility of safeguarding the interests of the African people, were faced with this conflict between the law and our conscience. In the face of the complete failure of the Government to heed, to consider, or even to respond to our seriously proposed objections and our solutions to the forthcoming Republic, what were we to do? Were we to allow the law which states that you shall not commit an offence by way of protest, to take its course and thus betray our conscience and our belief? Were we to uphold our conscience and our beliefs to strive for what we believe is right, not just for us, but for all the people who live in this country, both the present generation and for generations to come, and thus transgress against the law? This is the dilemma which faced us and in such a dilemma, men of honesty, men of purpose, and men of public morality and of conscience can only have one answer. They must follow the dictates of their conscience irrespective of the consequences which might overtake them for it. We of the Action Council, and I particularly as Secretary, followed my conscience.

If I had my time over I would do the same again, so would any man who dares call himself a man. We went ahead with our campaign as instructed by the conference and in accordance with its decisions.

The issue that sharply divided white South Africans during the referendum for a Republic did not interest us. It formed no part in our campaign. Continued association with the British monarchy on the one hand, or the establishment of a Boer Republic on the other—this was the crucial issue in so far as the White population was concerned and as it was put to them in the referendum. We are neither monarchists nor admirers of a Voortrekker type of republic. We believe that we were inspired by aspirations more worthy than either of the groups who took part in the campaign on these. We were inspired by the idea of bringing into being a democratic republic where all South Africans will enjoy human rights without the slightest discrimination; where African and non-African would be able to live together in peace, sharing a common nationality and a common loyalty to this country, which is our homeland. For these reasons we were opposed to the type of republic proposed by the Nationalist Party Government, just as we have been opposed previously to the constitutional basis of the Union of South Africa as a part of the British Empire. We were not prepared to accept, at a time when constitutional changes were being made, that these constitutional changes should not affect the real basis of a South African constitution, white supremacy and white domination, the very basis which has brought South Africa and its constitution into contempt and disrepute throughout the world.

I wish now to deal with the campaign itself, with the character of the campaign, and with the course of events which followed our decision. From the beginning our campaign was a campaign designed to call on people as a last extreme, if all else failed, if all discussions failed to materialize, if the Government showed no sign of taking any steps to attempt, either to treat with us or to meet our demands peacefully, to strike, that is to stay away from work, and so to bring economic pressure to bear. There was never any intention that our demonstrations, at that stage, go further than that. In all our statements, both those which are before the Court, and those which are not before the Court, we made it clear that that strike would be a peaceful protest, in which people were asked to remain in their homes. It was our intention that the demonstration should go through peacefully and peaceably, without clash and conflict, as such demonstrations do in every civilized country.

Nevertheless, around that campaign and our preparations for that campaign was created the atmosphere for civil war and revolution. I would say deliberately created. Deliberately created, not by us, Your Worship, but by the Government, which set out, from the beginning of this campaign, not to treat with us, not to heed us, not to talk to us, but rather to present us as wild, dangerous revolutionaries, intent on disorder and riot, incapable of being dealt with in any way save by mustering an overwhelming force against us and the implementation of every possible forcible means, legal and illegal, to suppress us. The Government behaved in a way no civilized government should dare behave when faced with a peaceful, disciplined, sensible, and democratic expression of the views of its own population. It ordered the mobilization of its armed forces to attempt to cow and terrorize our peaceful protest. It arrested people known to be active in African politics and in support of African demands for democratic rights, passed special laws enabling it to hold them without trial for twelve days instead of the forty-eight hours which had been customary before, and hold them, the majority of them, never to be charged before the courts, but to be released after the date for the strike had passed. If there was a danger during this period that violence would result from the situation in the country, then the possibility was of the Government's making. They set the scene for violence by relying exclusively on violence with which to answer our people and their demands. The countermeasures which they took clearly reflected growing uneasiness on their part, which grew out of the knowledge that their policy did not enjoy the support of the majority of the people, while ours did. It was clear that the Government was attempting to combat the intensity of our campaign by a reign of terror. At the time the newspapers suggested the strike was a failure and it was said that we did not enjoy the support of the people. I deny that. I deny it and I will continue to deny it as long as this Government is not prepared to put to the test the question of the opinion of the African people by consulting them in a democratic way. In any event the evidence in this case has shown that it was a substantial success. Our campaign was an intensive campaign and met with tremendous and overwhelming response from the population. In the end, if a strike did not materialize on the scale on which it had been hoped it would, it was not because the people were not willing, but because the overwhelming strength, violence, and force of the Government's attack against our campaign had for the time being achieved its aim of forcing us into submission against our wishes and against our conscience.

I wish again to return to the question of why people like me, knowing all this, knowing in advance that this Government is incapable of progressive democratic moves, so far as our people are concerned, knowing that this Government is incapable of reacting towards us in any way other than by the use of overwhelming brute force, why I, and people like me, nevertheless, decide to go ahead to do what we must do. We have been conditioned to our attitudes by the history which is not of our making. We have been conditioned by the history of White governments in this country to accept the fact that Africans, when they make their demands strongly and powerfully enough to have some chance of success, will be met by force and terror on the part of the Government. This is not something we have taught the African people, this is something the African people have learned from their own bitter experience. We learned it from each successive government. We learned it from the Government of General Smuts at the time of two massacres of our people: the 1921 massacre in Bulhoek when more than 100 men, women, and children were killed, and from the 1924 massacre—the Bondelswart massacre in South-West Africa, in which some 200 Africans were killed. We have continued to learn it from every successive Government.

Government violence can do only one thing and that is to breed counter-violence. We have warned repeatedly that the Government, by resorting continually to violence, will breed, in this country, counter-violence amongst the people, till ultimately, if there is no dawning of sanity on the part of the Government—ultimately, the dispute between the Government and my people will finish up by being settled in violence and by force. Already there are indications in this country that people, my people, Africans, are turning to deliberate acts of violence and of force against the Government, in order to persuade the Government, in the only language which this Government shows, by its own behaviour, that it understands.

Elsewhere in the world, a court would say to me, 'You should have made representations to the Government.' This Court, I am confident, will not say so. Representations have been made, by people who have gone before me, time and time again. Representations were made in this case by me; I do not want again to repeat the experience of those representations. The Court cannot expect a respect for the processes of representation and negotiation to grow amongst the African people, when the Government shows every day, by its conduct, that

23

it despises such processes and frowns upon them and will not indulge in them. Nor will the Court, I believe, say that, under the circumstances, my people are condemned forever to say nothing and to do nothing. If this Court says that, or believes it, I think it is mistaken and deceiving itself. Men are not capable of doing nothing, of saying nothing, of not reacting to injustice, of not protesting against oppression, of not striving for the good society and the good life in the ways they see it. Nor will they do so in this country.

Perhaps the Court will say that despite our human rights to protest, to object, to make ourselves heard, we should stay within the letter of the law. I would say, Sir, that it is the Government, its administration of the law, which brings the law into such contempt and disrepute that one is no longer concerned in this country to stay within the letter of the law. I will illustrate this from my own experience. The Government has used the process of law to handicap me, in my personal life, in my career, and in my political work, in a way which is calculated, in my opinion, to bring about a contempt for the law. In December 1952 I was issued with an order by the Government, not as a result of a trial before a court and a conviction, but as a result of prejudice, or perhaps Star Chamber procedure behind closed doors in the halls of Government. In terms of that order I was confined to the magisterial district of Johannesburg for six months and, at the same time, I was prohibited from attending gatherings for a similar period. That order expired in June 1953 and three months thereafter, again without any hearing, without any attempt to hear my side of the case, without facing me with charges, or explanations, both bans were renewed for a further period of two years. To these bans a third was added: I was ordered by the Minister of Justice to resign altogether from the African National Congress, and never again to become a member or to participate in its activities. Towards the end of 1955, I found myself free and able to move around once again, but not for long. In February 1956 the bans were again renewed, administratively, again without hearing, this time for five years. Again, by order of the Government, in the name of the law, I found myself restricted and isolated from my fellow men, from people who think like me and believe like me. I found myself trailed by officers of the Security Branch of the Police Force wherever I went. In short I found myself treated as a criminal—an unconvicted criminal. I was not allowed to pick my company, to frequent the company of men, to participate in their political activities, to join their organizations. I was not free from constant police surveillance. I was made, by the law, a criminal, not because of what I had done, but because of what I stood for, because of what I thought, because of my conscience. Can it be any wonder to anybody that such conditions make a man an outlaw of society? Can it be wondered that such a man, having been outlawed by the Government, should be prepared to lead the life of an outlaw, as I have led for some months, according to the evidence before this Court?

It has not been easy for me during the past period to separate myself from my wife and children, to say goodbye to the good old days when, at the end of a strenuous day at an office, I could look forward to joining my family at the dinner-table, and instead to take up the life of a man hunted continuously by the police, living separated from those who are closest to me, in my own country, facing continually the hazards of detection and of arrest. This has been a life infinitely more difficult than serving a prison sentence. No man in his right senses would voluntarily choose such a life in preference to the one of normal, family, social life which exists in every civilized community.

But there comes a time, as it came in my life, when a man is denied the right to live a normal life, when he can only live the life of an outlaw because the Government has so decreed to use the law to impose a state of outlawry upon him. I was driven to this situation, and I do not regret having taken the decisions that I did take. Other people will be driven in the same way in this country, by this very same force of police persecution and of administrative action by the Government, to follow my course, of that I am certain. The decision that I should continue to carry out the decisions of the Pietermaritzburg conference, despite police persecution all the time, was not my decision alone. It was a decision reached by me, in consultation with those who were entrusted with the leadership of the campaign and its fulfilment. It was clear to us then, in the early periods of the campaign, when the Government was busy whipping up an atmosphere of hysteria as the prelude to violence, that the views of the African people would not be heard, would not find expression, unless attempts were made deliberately by those of us entrusted with the task of carrying through the strike call to keep away from the illegal, unlawful attacks of the Special Branch, the unlawful detention of people for twelve days without trial, and unlawful and illegal intervention by the police and the Government forces in legitimate political activity of the population. I was, at the time of the Pietermaritzburg conference, free from bans for a short time, and a time which I had no reason to expect would prolong itself for very long. Had I remained in my normal surroundings, carrying on my normal life, I would have again been forced by Government action to a position of an outlaw. That I was not prepared to do while the commands of the Pietermaritzburg conference to me remained unfulfilled. New situations require new tactics. The situation, which was not of our making, which followed the Pietermaritzburg conference required the tactics which I adopted, I believe, correctly.

A lot has been written since the Pietermaritzburg conference, and even more since my arrest, much of which is flattering to my pride and dear to my heart, but much of which is mistaken and incorrect. It has been suggested that the advances, the articulateness of our people, the successes which they are achieving here, and the recognition which they are winning both here and abroad are in some way the result of my work. I must place on record my belief that I have been only one in a large army of people, to all of whom the credit for any success of achievement is due. Advance and progress is not the result of my work alone, but of the collective work of my colleagues and I, both here and abroad. I have been fortunate throughout my political life to work together with colleagues whose abilities and contributions to the cause of my people's freedom have been greater and better than my own, people who have been loved and respected by the African population generally as a result of the dedicated way in which they have fought for freedom and for peace and justice in this country. It distresses me to read reports that my arrest has been instigated by some of my colleagues for some sinister purposes of their own. Nothing could be further from the truth. I dismiss these suggestions as the sensational inventions of unscrupulous journalists. People who stoop to such unscrupulous manoeuvers as the betrayal of their own comrades have no place in the good fight which I have fought for the freedom of the African people, which my colleagues continue to fight without me today. Not just I alone, but all of us are willing to pay the penalties which we may have to pay, which I may have to pay for having followed my conscience in pursuit of what I believe is right. So are we all. Many people in this country have paid the price before me, and many will pay the price after me.

I do not believe, Your Worship, that this Court, in inflicting penalties on me for the crimes for which I am convicted, should be moved by the belief that penalties deter men from the course that they believe is right. History shows that penalties do not deter men when their conscience is aroused, nor will they deter my people or the colleagues with whom I have worked before.

I am prepared to pay the penalty even though I know how bitter and desperate is the situation of an African in the prisons of this country. I have been in these prisons and I know how gross is the discrimination, even behind the prison walls, against Africans, how much worse is the treatment meted out to African prisoners than that accorded to whites. Nevertheless, these considerations do not sway me from the path that I have taken, nor will they sway others like me. For to men, freedom in their own land is the pinnacle of their ambitions, from which nothing can turn men of conviction aside. More powerful than my fear of the dreadful conditions to which I might be subjected is my hatred for the dreadful conditions to which my people are subjected outside prison throughout this country.

I hate the practice of race discrimination, and in my hatred I am sustained by the fact that the overwhelming majority of mankind hate it equally. I hate the systematic inculcation of children with colour prejudice and I am sustained in that hatred by the fact that the overwhelming majority of mankind, here and abroad, are with me in that. I hate the racial arrogance which decrees that the good things of life shall be retained as the exclusive right of a minority of the population, and which reduces the majority of the population to a position of subservience and inferiority, and maintains them as voteless chattels to work where they are told and behave as they are told by the ruling minority. I am sustained in that hatred by the fact that the overwhelming majority of mankind both in this country and abroad are with me.

Nothing that this Court can do to me will change in any way that hatred in me, which can only be removed by the removal of the injustice and the inhumanity which I have sought to remove from the political, social, and life of this country.

Whatever sentence Your Worship sees fit to impose upon me for the crime for which I have been convicted before this Court, may it rest assured that when my sentence has been completed, I will still be moved, as men are always moved, by their consciences; I will still be moved by my dislike of the race discrimination against my people when I come out from serving my sentence, to take up again, as best I can, the struggle for the removal of those injustices until they are finally abolished once and for all.

I now wish to deal with the Second Count.

When my colleagues and I received the invitation to attend the Conference of the Pan-African Freedom Movement for East and Central Africa, it was decided that I should leave the country and join our delegation to Addis Ababa, the capital of Ethiopia, where the conference would be held. It was part of my mandate to tour Africa and make direct contact with African leaders on the continent.

I did not apply for a passport because I knew very well that it would not be granted to me. After all, the Nationalist Party Government, throughout the fourteen years of its oppressive role, had refused permission to leave the country to many African scholars, educationalists, artists, sportsmen, and clerics, and I wished to waste none of my time by applying for a passport.

The tour of the continent made a forceful impression on me. For the first time in my life I was a free man; free from white oppression, from the idiocy of apartheid and racial arrogance, from police molestation, from humiliation and indignity. Wherever I went I was treated like a human being. I met Rashidi Kawawa, Prime Minister of Tanganyika, and Julius Nyerere. I was received by Emperor Haile Selassie, by General Abboud, President of Sudan, by Habib Bourguiba, President of Tunisia, and by Modibo Keita of the Republic of Mali.

I met Léopold Senghor, President of Senegal, Presidents Sékou Touré and Tubman, of Guinea and Liberia, respectively.

I met Ben Bella, the President of Algeria, and Colonel Boumedienne, the Commander-in-Chief of the Algerian Army of National Liberation. I saw the cream and flower of the Algerian youth who had fought French imperialism and whose valour had brought freedom and happiness to their country.

In London I was received by Hugh Gaitskell, Leader of the Labour Party, and by Jo Grimond, Leader of the Liberal Party, and other prominent Englishmen.

I met Prime Minister Obote of Uganda, distinguished African nationalists like Kenneth Kaunda, Oginga Odinga, Joshua Nkomo, and many others. In all these countries we were showered with hospitality, and assured of solid support for our cause.

In its efforts to keep the African people in a position of perpetual subordination, South Africa must and will fail. South Africa is out of step with the rest of the

27

civilized world, as is shown by the resolution adopted last night by the General Assembly of the United Nations Organization which decided to impose diplomatic and economic sanctions. In the African States, I saw black and white mingling peacefully and happily in hotels, cinemas, trading in the same areas, using the same public transport, and living in the same residential areas.

I had to return home to report to my colleagues and to share my impressions and experiences with them.

I have done my duty to my people and to South Africa. I have no doubt that posterity will pronounce that I was innocent and that the criminals that should have been brought before this Court are the members of the Verwoerd Government.

Mandela was sentenced to three years' imprisonment on the charge of incitement and two years' for leaving the country without valid travel documents.

THE RIVONIA TRIAL, 1963-4
"I AM PREPARED TO DIE"

Mandela's statement from the dock in Pretoria Supreme Court, 20 April 1964 at the opening of the defence case.

I am the First Accused.

I hold a Bachelor's Degree in Arts and practised as an attorney in Johannesburg for a number of years in partnership with Oliver Tambo. I am a convicted prisoner serving five years for leaving the country without a permit and for inciting people to go on strike at the end of May 1961.

At the outset, I want to say that the suggestion made by the State in its opening that the struggle in South Africa is under the influence of foreigners or communists is wholly incorrect. I have done whatever I did, both as an individual and as a leader of my people, because of my experience in South Africa and my own proudly felt African background, and not because of what any outsider might have said.

In my youth in the Transkei I listened to the elders of my tribe telling stories of the old days. Amongst the tales they related to me were those of wars fought by our ancestors in defence of the fatherland. The names of Dingane and Bambata, Hintsa and Makana, Squngthi and Dalasile, Moshoeshoe and Sekhukhuni, were praised as the glory of the entire African nation. I hoped then that life might offer me the opportunity to serve my people and make my own humble contribution to their freedom struggle. This is what has motivated me in all that I have done in relation to the charges made against me in this case.

Having said this, I must deal immediately and at some length with the question of violence. Some of the things so far told to the Court are true and some are untrue. I do not, however, deny that I planned sabotage. I did not plan it in a spirit of recklessness, nor because I have any love of violence. I planned it as a result of a calm and sober assessment of the political situation that had arisen after many years of tyranny, exploitation, and oppression of my people by the Whites.

I admit immediately that I was one of the persons who helped to form Umkhonto we Sizwe, and that I played a prominent role in its affairs until I was arrested in August 1962.

In the statement which I am about to make I shall correct certain false impressions which have been created by State witnesses. Amongst other things, I will demonstrate that certain of the acts referred to in the evidence were not and could not have been committed by Umkhonto. I will also deal with the relationship between the African National Congress and Umkhonto, and with the part which I personally have played in the affairs of both organizations. I shall deal also with the part played by the Communist Party. In order to explain these matters properly, I will have to explain what Umkhonto set out to achieve; what methods it prescribed for the achievement of these objects, and why these methods were chosen. I will also have to explain how I became involved in the activities of these organizations.

I deny that Umkhonto was responsible for a number of acts which clearly fell outside the policy of the organization, and which have been charged in the indictment against us. I do not know what justification there was for these acts, but to demonstrate that they could not have been authorized by Umkhonto, I want to refer briefly to the roots and policy of the organization.

I have already mentioned that I was one of the persons who helped to form Umkhonto. I, and the others who started the organization, did so for two reasons. Firstly, we believed that as a result of Government policy, violence by the African people had become inevitable, and that unless responsible leadership was given to canalize and control the feelings of our people, there would be outbreaks of terrorism which would produce an intensity of bitterness and hostility between the various races of this country which is not produced even by war. Secondly, we felt that without violence there would be no way open to the African people to succeed in their struggle against the principle of white supremacy. All lawful modes of expressing opposition to this principle had been closed by legislation, and we were placed in a position in which we had either to accept a permanent state of inferiority, or to defy the Government. We chose to defy the law. We first broke the law in a way which avoided any recourse to violence; when this form was legislated against, and then the Government resorted to a show of force to crush opposition to its policies, only then did we decide to answer violence with violence.

But the violence which we chose to adopt was not terrorism. We who formed Umkhonto were all members of the African National Congress, and had behind us the ANC tradition of non-violence and negotiation as a means of solving political disputes. We believe that South Africa belongs to all the people who live in it, and not to one group, be it black or white. We did not want an inter-racial war, and tried to avoid it to the last minute. If the Court is in doubt about this, it will be seen that the whole history of our organization bears out what I have said, and what I will subsequently say, when I describe the tactics which Umkhonto decided to adopt. I want, therefore, to say something about the African National Congress.

The African National Congress was formed in 1912 to defend the rights of the African people which had been seriously curtailed by the South Africa Act, and which were then being threatened by the Native Land Act. For thirty-seven years—that is until 1949—it adhered strictly to a constitutional struggle. It put forward demands and resolutions; it sent delegations to the Government in the belief that African grievances could be settled through peaceful discussion and that Africans could advance gradually to full political rights. But White Governments remained unmoved, and the rights of Africans became less instead of becoming greater. In the words of my leader, Chief Lutuli, who became President of the ANC in 1952, and who was later awarded the Nobel Peace Prize:

"who will deny that thirty years of my life have been spent knocking in vain, patiently, moderately, and modestly at a closed and barred door? What have been the fruits of moderation? The past thirty years have seen the greatest number of laws restricting our rights and progress, until today we have reached a stage where we have almost no rights at all".

Even after 1949, the ANC remained determined to avoid violence. At this time, however, there was a change from the strictly constitutional means of protest which had been employed in the past. The change was embodied in a decision which was taken to protest against apartheid legislation by peaceful, but unlawful, demonstrations against certain laws. Pursuant to this policy the ANC launched the Defiance Campaign, in which I was placed in charge of volunteers. This campaign was based on the principles of passive resistance. More than 8,500 people defied apartheid laws and went to jail. Yet there was not a single instance of violence in the course of this campaign on the part of any defier. I and nineteen colleagues were convicted for the role which we played in organizing the campaign, but our sentences were suspended mainly because the Judge found that discipline and non-violence had been stressed throughout. This was the time when the volunteer section of the ANC was established, and when the word 'Amadelakufa'* was first used: this was the time when the volunteers were asked to take a pledge to uphold certain principles. Evidence dealing with volunteers and their pledges has been introduced into this case, but completely out of context. The volunteers were not, and are not, the soldiers of a black army pledged to fight a civil war against the whites. They were, and are, dedicated workers who are prepared to lead campaigns initiated by the ANC to distribute leaflets, to organize strikes, or do whatever

---

*Amadelakufa = those who are prepared to make sacrifices.

the particular campaign required. They are called volunteers because they volunteer to face the penalties of imprisonment and whipping which are now prescribed by the legislature for such acts.

During the Defiance Campaign, the Public Safety Act and the Criminal Law Amendment Act were passed. These Statutes provided harsher penalties for offences committed by way of protests against laws. Despite this, the protests continued and the ANC adhered to its policy of non-violence. In 1956, 156 leading members of the Congress Alliance, including myself, were arrested on a charge of high treason and charges under the Suppression of Communism Act. The non-violent policy of the ANC was put in issue by the State, but when the Court gave judgement some five years later, it found that the ANC did not have a policy of violence. We were acquitted on all counts, which included a count that the ANC sought to set up a communist state in place of the existing regime. The Government has always sought to label all its opponents as communists. This allegation has been repeated in the present case, but as I will show, the ANC is not, and never has been, a communist organization.

In 1960 there was the shooting at Sharpeville, which resulted in the proclamation of a state of emergency and the declaration of the ANC as an unlawful organization. My colleagues and I, after careful consideration, decided that we would not obey this decree. The African people were not part of the Government and did not make the laws by which they were governed. We believed in the words of the Universal Declaration of Human Rights, that 'the will of the people shall be the basis of authority of the Government', and for us to accept the banning was equivalent to accepting the silencing of the Africans for all time. The ANC refused to dissolve, but instead went underground. We believed it was our duty to preserve this organization which had been built up with almost fifty years of unremitting toil. I have no doubt that no self-respecting White political organization would disband itself if declared illegal by a government in which it had no say.

In 1960 the Government held a referendum which led to the establishment of the Republic. Africans, who constituted approximately 70 per cent of the population of South Africa, were not entitled to vote, and were not even consulted about the proposed constitutional change. All of us were apprehensive of our future under the proposed White Republic, and a resolution was taken to hold an All-In African Conference to call for a National Convention, and to organize mass demonstrations on the eve of the unwanted Republic, if the Government failed to call the Convention. The conference was attended by Africans of various political persuasions. I was the Secretary of the conference and undertook to be responsible for organizing the national stay-at-home which was subsequently called to coincide with the declaration of the Republic. As all strikes by Africans are illegal, the person organizing such a strike must avoid arrest. I was chosen to be this person, and consequently I had to leave my home and family and my practice and go into hiding to avoid arrest.

31

The stay-at-home, in accordance with ANC policy, was to be a peaceful demonstration. Careful instructions were given to organizers and members to avoid any recourse to violence. The Government's answer was to introduce new and harsher laws, to mobilize its armed forces, and to send Saracens*, armed vehicles, and soldiers into the townships in a massive show of force designed to intimidate the people. This was an indication that the Government had decided to rule by force alone, and this decision was a milestone on the road to Umkhonto.

Some of this may appear irrelevant to this trial. In fact, I believe none of it is irrelevant because it will, I hope, enable the Court to appreciate the attitude eventually adopted by the various persons and bodies concerned in the National Liberation Movement. When I went to jail in 1962, the dominant idea was that loss of life should be avoided. I now know that this was still so in 1963.

I must return to June 1961. What were we, the leaders of our people, to do? Were we to give in to the show of force and the implied threat against future action, or were we to fight it and, if so, how?

We had no doubt that we had to continue the fight. Anything else would have been abject surrender. Our problem was not whether to fight, but was how to continue the fight. We of the ANC had always stood for a non-racial democracy, and we shrank from any action which might drive the races further apart than they already were. But the hard facts were that fifty years of non-violence had brought the African people nothing but more and more repressive legislation, and fewer and fewer rights. It may not be easy for this Court to understand, but it is a fact that for a long time the people had been talking of violence—of the day when they would fight the White man and win back their country—and we, the leaders of the ANC, had nevertheless always prevailed upon them to avoid violence and to pursue peaceful methods. When some of us discussed this in May and June of 1961, it could not be denied that our policy to achieve a non-racial State by non-violence had achieved nothing, and that our followers were beginning to lose confidence in this policy and were developing disturbing ideas of terrorism.

It must not be forgotten that by this time violence had, in fact, become a feature of the South African political scene. There had been violence in 1957 when the women of Zeerust were ordered to carry passes; there was violence in 1958 with the enforcement of cattle culling in Sekhukhuniland; there was violence in 1959 when the people of Cato Manor protested against pass raids; there was violence in 1960 when the Government attempted to impose Bantu Authorities in Pondoland. Thirty-nine Africans died in these disturbances. In 1961 there had been riots in Warmbaths, and all this time the Transkei had been a seething mass of unrest. Each disturbance pointed clearly to the inevitable growth among Africans of the belief that violence was the only way out—it showed that a Government which uses force to maintain its rule teaches the

---

*Saracen armoured vehicles: British-made military troop carriers.

oppressed to use force to oppose it. Already small groups had arisen in the urban areas and were spontaneously making plans for violent forms of political struggle. There now arose a danger that these groups would adopt terrorism against Africans, as well as Whites, if not properly directed. Particularly disturbing was the type of violence engendered in places such as Zeerust, Sekhukhuniland, and Pondoland amongst Africans. It was increasingly taking the form, not of struggle against the Government—though this is what prompted it—but of civil strife amongst themselves, conducted in such a way that it could not hope to achieve anything other than a loss of life and bitterness.

At the beginning of June 1961, after a long and anxious assessment of the South African situation, I, and some colleagues, came to the conclusion that as violence in this country was inevitable, it would be unrealistic and wrong for African leaders to continue preaching peace and non-violence at a time when the Government met our peaceful demands with force.

This conclusion was not easily arrived at. It was only when all else had failed, when all channels of peaceful protest had been barred to us, that the decision was made to embark on violent forms of political struggle, and to form Umkhonto we Sizwe. We did so not because we desired such a course, but solely because the Government had left us with no other choice. In the Manifesto of Umkhonto published on 16 December 1961, which is Exhibit AD, we said:

"The time comes in the life of any nation when there remain only two choices —submit or fight. That time has now come to South Africa. We shall not submit and we have no choice but to hit back by all means in our power in defence of our people, our future, and our freedom".

This was our feeling in June of 1961 when we decided to press for a change in the policy of the National Liberation Movement. I can only say that I felt morally obliged to do what I did.

We who had taken this decision started to consult leaders of various organizations, including the ANC. I will not say whom we spoke to, or what they said, but I wish to deal with the role of the African National Congress in this phase of the struggle, and with the policy and objectives of Umkhonto we Sizwe.

As far as the ANC was concerned, it formed a clear view which can be summarized as follows:

(a) It was a mass political organization with a political function to fulfil. Its members had joined on the express policy of non-violence.

(b) Because of all this, it could not and would not undertake violence. This must be stressed. One cannot turn such a body into the small, closely knit organization required for sabotage. Nor would this be politically correct, because it would result in members ceasing to carry out this essential activity: political propaganda and organization. Nor was it permissible to change the whole nature of the organization.

33

(c) On the other hand, in view of this situation I have described, the ANC was prepared to depart from its fifty-year-old policy of non-violence to this extent that it would no longer disapprove of properly controlled violence. Hence members who undertook such activity would not be subject to disciplinary action by the ANC.

I say 'properly controlled violence' because I made it clear that if I formed the organization I would at all times subject it to the political guidance of the ANC and would not undertake any different form of activity from that contemplated without the consent of the ANC. And I shall now tell the Court how that form of violence came to be determined.

As a result of this decision, Umkhonto was formed in November 1961. When we took this decision, and subsequently formulated our plans, the ANC heritage of non-violence and racial harmony was very much with us. We felt that the country was drifting towards a civil war in which Blacks and Whites would fight each other. We viewed the situation with alarm. Civil war could mean the destruction of what the ANC stood for; with civil war, racial peace would be more difficult than ever to achieve. We already have examples in South African history of the results of war. It has taken more than fifty years for the scars of the South African War to disappear. How much longer would it take to eradicate the scars of inter-racial civil war, which could not be fought without a great loss of life on both sides ?

The avoidance of civil war had dominated our thinking for many years, but when we decided to adopt violence as part of our policy, we realized that we might one day have to face the prospect of such a war. This had to be taken into account in formulating our plans. We required a plan which was flexible and which permitted us to act in accordance with the needs of the times; above all, the plan had to be one which recognized civil war as the last resort, and left the decision on this question to the future. We did not want to be committed to civil war, but we wanted to be ready if it became inevitable.

Four forms of violence were possible. There is sabotage, there is guerrilla warfare, there is terrorism, and there is open revolution. We chose to adopt the first method and to exhaust it before taking any other decision.

In the light of our political background the choice was a logical one. Sabotage did not involve loss of life, and it offered the best hope for future race relations. Bitterness would be kept to a minimum and, if the policy bore fruit, democratic government could become a reality. This is what we felt at the time, and this is what we said in our Manifesto (Exhibit AD):

"We of Umkhonto We Sizwe have always sought to achieve liberation without bloodshed and civil clash. We hope, even at this late hour, that our first actions will awaken everyone to a realization of the disastrous situation to which the Nationalist policy is leading. We hope that we will bring the Government and its supporters to their senses before it is too late, so that both the Government and its policies can be changed before matters reach the desperate stage of civil war."

The initial plan was based on a careful analysis of the political and economic situation of our country. We believed that South Africa depended to a large extent on foreign capital and foreign trade. We felt that planned destruction of power plants, and interference with rail and telephone communications, would tend to scare away capital from the country, make it more difficult for goods from the industrial areas to reach the seaports on schedule, and would in the long run be a heavy drain on the economic life of the country, thus compelling the voters of the country to reconsider their position.

Attacks on the economic life lines of the country were to be linked with sabotage on Government buildings and other symbols of apartheid. These attacks would serve as a source of inspiration to our people. In addition, they would provide an outlet for those people who were urging the adoption of violent methods and would enable us to give concrete proof to our followers that we had adopted a stronger line and were fighting back against Government violence.

In addition, if mass action were successfully organized, and mass reprisals taken, we felt that sympathy for our cause would be roused in other countries, and that greater pressure would be brought to bear on the South African Government.

This then was the plan. Umkhonto was to perform sabotage, and strict instructions were given to its members right from the start, that on no account were they to injure or kill people in planning or carrying out operations. These instructions have been referred to in the evidence of 'Mr. X' and 'Mr. Z'.*

The affairs of the Umkhonto were controlled and directed by a National High Command, which had powers of co-option and which could, and did, appoint Regional Commands. The High Command was the body which determined tactics and targets and was in charge of training and finance. Under the High Command there were Regional Commands which were responsible for the direction of the local sabotage groups. Within the framework of the policy laid down by the National High Command, the Regional Commands had authority to select the targets to be attacked. They had no authority to go beyond the prescribed framework and thus had no authority to embark upon acts which endangered life, or which did not fit into the overall plan of sabotage. For instance, Umkhonto members were forbidden ever to go armed into operation. Incidentally, the terms High Command and Regional Command were an importation from the Jewish national underground organization Irgun Zvai Leumi, which operated in Israel between 1944 and 1948.

Umkhonto had its first operation on 16 December 1961, when Government buildings in Johannesburg, Port Elizabeth and Durban were attacked. The selection of targets is proof of the policy to which I have referred. Had we intended to attack life we would have selected targets where people congregated and not empty buildings and power stations. The sabotage which was committed before 16 December 1961 was the work of isolated groups and had no connection

---

*State witnesses in the trial whose names were withheld for their protection.

whatever with Umkhonto. In fact, some of these and a number of later acts were claimed by other organizations.

The Manifesto of Umkhonto was issued on the day that operations commenced. The response to our actions and Manifesto among the white population was characteristically violent. The Government threatened to take strong action, and called upon its supporters to stand firm and to ignore the demands of the Africans. The Whites failed to respond by suggesting change; they responded to our call by suggesting the laager.

In contrast, the response of the Africans was one of encouragement. Suddenly there was hope again. Things were happening. People in the townships became eager for political news. A great deal of enthusiasm was generated by the initial successes, and people began to speculate on how soon freedom would be obtained.

But we in Umkhonto weighed up the white response with anxiety. The lines were being drawn. The whites and blacks were moving into separate camps, and the prospects of avoiding a civil war were made less. The white newspapers carried reports that sabotage would be punished by death. If this was so, how could we continue to keep Africans away from terrorism?

Already scores of Africans had died as a result of racial friction. In 1920 when the famous leader, Masabala, was held in Port Elizabeth jail, twenty-four of a group of Africans who had gathered to demand his release were killed by the police and white civilians. In 1921, more than one hundred Africans died in the Bulhoek affair. In 1924 over two hundred Africans were killed when the Administrator of South-West Africa led a force against a group which had rebelled against the imposition of dog tax. On 1 May 1950, eighteen Africans died as a result of police shootings during the strike. On 21 March 1960, sixty-nine unarmed Africans died at Sharpeville.

How many more Sharpevilles would there be in the history of our country? And how many more Sharpevilles could the country stand without violence and terror becoming the order of the day? And what would happen to our people when that stage was reached? In the long run we felt certain we must succeed, but at what cost to ourselves and the rest of the country? And if this happened, how could black and white ever live together again in peace and harmony? These were the problems that faced us, and these were our decisions.

Experience convinced us that rebellion would offer the Government limitless opportunities for the indiscriminate slaughter of our people. But it was precisely because the soil of South Africa is already drenched with the blood of innocent Africans that we felt it our duty to make preparations as a long-term undertaking to use force in order to defend ourselves against force. If war were inevitable, we wanted the fight to be conducted on terms most favourable to our people. The fight which held out prospects best for us and the least risk of life to both sides was guerrilla warfare. We decided, therefore, in our preparations for the future, to make provision for the possibility of guerrilla warfare.

All whites undergo compulsory military training, but no such training was given to Africans. It was in our view essential to build up a nucleus of trained men who would be able to provide the leadership which would be required if guerrilla warfare started. We had to prepare for such a situation before it became too late to make proper preparations. It was also necessary to build up a nucleus of men trained in civil administration and other professions, so that Africans would be equipped to participate in the government of this country as soon as they were allowed to do so.

At this stage it was decided that I should attend the Conference of the Pan-African Freedom Movement for Central, East, and Southern Africa, which was to be held early in 1962 in Addis Ababa, and, because of our need for preparation, it was also decided that, after the conference, I would undertake a tour of the African States with a view to obtaining facilities for the training of soldiers, and that I would also solicit scholarships for the higher education of matriculated Africans. Training in both fields would be necessary, even if changes came about by peaceful means. Administrators would be necessary who would be willing and able to administer a non-racial State and so would men be necessary to control the army and police force of such a State.

It was on this note that I left South Africa to proceed to Addis Ababa as a delegate of the ANC. My tour was a success. Wherever I went I met sympathy for our cause and promises of help. All Africa was united against the stand of White South Africa, and even in London I was received with great sympathy by political leaders, such as Mr. Gaitskell and Mr. Grimond. In Africa I was promised support by such men as Julius Nyerere, now President of Tanganyika; Mr. Kawawa, then Prime Minister of Tanganyika; Emperor Haile Selassie of Ethiopia; General Abboud, President of the Sudan; Habib Bourguiba, President of Tunisia; Ben Bella, now President of Algeria; Modibo Keita, President of Mali; Leopold Senghor, President of Senegal; Sékou Touré, President of Guinea; President Tubman of Liberia; and Milton Obote, Prime Minister of Uganda. It was Ben Bella who invited me to visit Oujda, the Headquarters of the Algerian Army of National Liberation, the visit which is described in my diary, one of the Exhibits.

I started to make a study of the art of war and revolution and, whilst abroad, underwent a course in military training. If there was to be guerrilla warfare, I wanted to be able to stand and fight with my people and to share the hazards of war with them. Notes of lectures which I received in Algeria are contained in Exhibit 16, produced in evidence. Summaries of books on guerrilla warfare and military strategy have also been produced. I have already admitted that these documents are in my writing, and I acknowledge that I made these studies to equip myself for the role which I might have to play if the struggle drifted into guerrilla warfare. I approached this question as every African Nationalist should do. I was completely objective. The Court will see that I attempted to examine all types of authority on the subject—from the East and from the West, going back to the classic work of Clausewitz, and covering such a variety as Mao Tse

Tung and Che Guevara on the one hand, and the writings on the Anglo-Boer War on the other. Of course, these notes are merely summaries of the books I read and do not contain my personal views.

I also made arrangements for our recruits to undergo military training. But here it was impossible to organize any scheme without the co-operation of the ANC offices in Africa. I consequently obtained the permission of the ANC in South Africa to do this. To this extent then there was a departure from the original decision of the ANC, but it applied outside South Africa only. The first batch of recruits actually arrived in Tanganyika when I was passing through that country on my way back to South Africa.

I returned to South Africa and reported to my colleagues on the results of my trip. On my return I found that there had been little alteration in the political scene save that the threat of a death penalty for sabotage had now become a fact. The attitude of my colleagues in Umkhonto was much the same as it had been before I left. They were feeling their way cautiously and felt that it would be a long time before the possibilities of sabotage were exhausted. In fact, the view was expressed by some that the training of recruits was premature. This is recorded by me in the document which is Exhibit R.14. After a full discussion, however, it was decided to go ahead with the plans for military training because of the fact that it would take many years to build up a sufficient nucleus of trained soldiers to start a guerrilla campaign, and whatever happened the training would be of value.

I wish to turn now to certain general allegations made in this case by the State. But before doing so, I wish to revert to certain occurrences said by witnesses to have happened in Port Elizabeth and East London. I am referring to the bombing of private houses of pro-Government persons during September, October and November 1962. I do not know what justification there was for these acts, nor what provocation had been given. But if what I have said already is accepted, then it is clear that these acts had nothing to do with the carrying out of the policy of Umkhonto.

One of the chief allegations in the indictment is that the ANC was a party to a general conspiracy to commit sabotage. I have already explained why this is incorrect but how, externally, there was a departure from the original principle laid down by the ANC. There has, of course, been overlapping of functions internally as well, because there is a difference between a resolution adopted in the atmosphere of a committee room and the concrete difficulties that arise in the field of practical activity. At a later stage the position was further affected by bannings and house arrests, and by persons leaving the country to take up political work abroad. This led to individuals having to do work in different capacities. But though this may have blurred the distinction between Umkhonto and the ANC, it by no means abolished that distinction. Great care was taken to keep the activities of the two organizations in South Africa distinct. The ANC remained a mass political body of Africans only carrying on the type of political work they had conducted prior to 1961. Umkhonto remained a small organization recruiting its members from different races and organizations and trying to achieve its own particular object. The fact that members of Umkhonto were recruited from the ANC, and the fact that persons served both organizations, like Solomon Mbanjwa, did not, in our view, change the nature of the ANC or give it a policy of violence. This overlapping of officers, however, was more the exception than the rule. This is why persons such as 'Mr. X' and 'Mr. Z', who were on the Regional Command of their respective areas, did not participate in any of the ANC committees or activities, and why people such as Mr. Bennett Mashiyana and Mr. Reginald Ndubi did not hear of sabotage at their ANC meetings.

Another of the allegations in the indictment is that Rivonia was the headquarters of Umkhonto. This is not true of the time when I was there. I was told, of course, and knew that certain of the activities of the Communist Party were carried on there. But this is no reason (as I shall presently explain) why I should not use the place.

I came there in the following manner:

(a) As already indicated, early in April 1961 I went underground to organize the May general strike. My work entailed travelling throughout the country, living now in African townships, then in country villages and again in cities.

   During the second half of the year I started visiting the Parktown home of Arthur Goldreich, where I used to meet my family privately. Although I had no direct political association with him, I had known Arthur Goldreich socially since 1958.*

(b) In October, Arthur Goldreich informed me that he was moving out of town and offered me a hiding place there. A few days thereafter, he arranged for Michael Harmel to take me to Rivonia. I naturally found Rivonia an ideal place for the man who lived the life of an outlaw. Up to that time I had been compelled to live indoors during the daytime and could only venture out under cover of darkness. But at Liliesleaf** [farm, Rivonia,] I could live differently and work far more efficiently.

(c) For obvious reasons, I had to disguise myself and I assumed the fictitious name of David. In December, Arthur Goldreich and his family moved in. I stayed there until I went abroad on 11 January 1962. As already indicated, I returned in July 1962 and was arrested in Natal on 5 August.

(d) Up to the time of my arrest, Liliesleaf farm was the headquarters of neither the African National Congress nor Umkhonto. With the exception of myself, none of the officials or members of these bodies lived there, no meetings of the governing bodies were ever held there, and no activities

---

*Arthur Goldreich was among those arrested in connection with the Rivonia case. Later he and three others in custody escaped from jail by bribing a guard, and fled the country.
**Liliesleaf was the name of the farm in the district of Rivonia on the northern outskirts of Johannesburg where the arrests took place. At the time it was let to Arthur Goldreich.

connected with them were either organized or directed from there. On numerous occasions during my stay at Liliesleaf farm I met both the Executive Committee of the ANC, as well as the NHC, but such meetings were held elsewhere and not on the farm.

(e) Whilst staying at Liliesleaf farm, I frequently visited Arthur Goldreich in the main house and he also paid me visits in my room. We had numerous political discussions covering a variety of subjects. We discussed ideological and practical questions, the Congress Alliance, Umkhonto and its activities generally, and his experiences as a soldier in the Palmach, the military wing of the Haganah. Haganah was the political authority of the Jewish National Movement in Palestine.

(f) Because of what I had got to know of Goldreich, I recommended on my return to South Africa that he should be recruited to Umkhonto. I do not know of my personal knowledge whether this was done.

Another of the allegations made by the State is that the aims and objects of the ANC and the Communist Party are the same. I wish to deal with this and with my own political position, because I must assume that the State may try to argue from certain Exhibits that I tried to introduce Marxism into the ANC. The allegation as to the ANC is false. This is an old allegation which was disproved at the Treason Trial and which has again reared its head. But since the allegation has been made again, I shall deal with it as well as with the relationship between the ANC and the Communist Party and Umkhonto and that party.

The ideological creed of the ANC is, and always has been, the creed of African Nationalism. It is not the concept of African Nationalism expressed in the cry, 'Drive the White man into the sea'. The African Nationalism for which the ANC stands is the concept of freedom and fulfilment for the African people in their own land. The most important political document ever adopted by the ANC is the 'Freedom Charter'. It is by no means a blueprint for a socialist state. It calls for redistribution, but not nationalization, of land; it provides for nationalization of mines, banks, and monopoly industry, because big monopolies are owned by one race only, and without such nationalization racial domination would be perpetuated despite the spread of political power. It would be a hollow gesture to repeal the Gold Law prohibitions against Africans when all gold mines are owned by European companies. In this respect the ANC's policy corresponds with the old policy of the present Nationalist Party which, for many years, had as part of its programme the nationalization of the gold mines which, at that time, were controlled by foreign capital. Under the Freedom Charter, nationalization would take place in an economy based on private enterprise. The realization of the Freedom Charter would open up fresh fields for a prosperous African population of all classes, including the middle class. The ANC has never at any period of its history advocated a revolutionary change in the economic structure of the country, nor has it, to the best of my recollection, ever condemned capitalist society.

As far as the Communist Party is concerned, and if I understand its policy correctly, it stands for the establishment of a State based on the principles of Marxism. Although it is prepared to work for the Freedom Charter, as a short-term solution to the problems created by white supremacy, it regards the Freedom Charter as the beginning, and not the end, of its programme.

The ANC, unlike the Communist Party, admitted Africans only as members. Its chief goal was, and is, for the African people to win unity and full political rights. The Communist Party's main aim, on the other hand, was to remove the capitalists and to replace them with a working-class government. The Communist Party sought to emphasize class distinctions whilst the ANC seeks to harmonize them. This is a vital distinction.

It is true that there has often been close co-operation between the ANC and the Communist Party. But co-operation is merely proof of a common goal—in this case the removal of white supremacy—and is not proof of a complete community of interests.

The history of the world is full of similar examples. Perhaps the most striking illustration is to be found in the co-operation between Great Britain, the United States of America, and the Soviet Union in the fight against Hitler. Nobody but Hitler would have dared to suggest that such co-operation turned Churchill or Roosevelt into communists or communist tools, or that Britain and America were working to bring about a communist world.

Another instance of such co-operation is to be found precisely in Umkhonto. Shortly after Umkhonto was constituted, I was informed by some of its members that the Communist Party would support Umkhonto, and this then occurred. At a later stage the support was made openly.

I believe that communists have always played an active role in the fight by colonial countries for their freedom, because the short-term objects of communism would always correspond with the long-term objects of freedom movements. Thus communists have played an important role in the freedom struggles fought in countries such as Malaya, Algeria, and Indonesia, yet none of these States today are communist countries. Similarly in the underground resistance movements which sprung up in Europe during the last World War, communists played an important role. Even General Chiang Kai-Shek, today one of the bitterest enemies of communism, fought together with the communists against the ruling class in the struggle which led to his assumption of power in China in the 1930s.

This pattern of co-operation between communists and non-communists has been repeated in the National Liberation Movement of South Africa. Prior to the banning of the Communist Party, joint campaigns involving the Communist Party and the Congress movements were accepted practice. African communists could, and did, become members of the ANC, and some served on the National, Provincial, and local committees. Amongst those who served on the National Executive are Albert Nzula, a former Secretary of the Communist Party, Moses

Kotane, another former Secretary, and J. B. Marks, a former member of the Central Committee.

I joined the ANC in 1944, and in my younger days I held the view that the policy of admitting communists to the ANC, and the close co-operation which existed at times on specific issues between the ANC and the Communist Party, would lead to a watering down of the concept of African Nationalism. At that stage I was a member of the African National Congress Youth League, and was one of a group which moved for the expulsion of communists from the ANC. This proposal was heavily defeated. Amongst those who voted against the proposal were some of the most conservative sections of African political opinion. They defended the policy on the ground that from its inception the ANC was formed and built up, not as a political party with one school of political thought, but as a Parliament of the African people, accommodating people ot various political convictions, all united by the common goal of national liberation. I was eventually won over to this point of view and I have upheld it ever since.

It is perhaps difficult for white South Africans, with an ingrained prejudice against communism, to understand why experienced African politicians so readily accept communists as their friends. But to us the reason is obvious. Theoretical differences amongst those fighting against oppression is a luxury we cannot afford at this stage. What is more, for many decades communists were the only political group in South Africa who were prepared to treat Africans as human beings and their equals; who were prepared to eat with us; talk with us, live with us, and work with us. They were the only political group which was prepared to work with the Africans for the attainment of political rights and a stake in society. Because of this, there are many Africans who, today, tend to equate freedom with communism. They are supported in this belief by a legislature which brands all exponents of democratic government and African freedom as communists and bans many of them (who are not communists) under the Suppression of Communism Act. Although I have never been a member of the Communist Party, I myself have been named under that pernicious Act because of the role I played in the Defiance Campaign. I have also been banned and imprisoned under that Act.

It is not only in internal politics that we count communists as amongst those who support our cause. In the international field, communist countries have always come to our aid. In the United Nations and other Councils of the world the communist *bloc* has supported the Afro-Asian struggle against colonialism and often seems to be more sympathetic to our plight than some of the Western powers. Although there is a universal condemnation of apartheid, the communist *bloc* speaks out against it with a louder voice than most of the white world. In these circumstances, it would take a brash young politician, such as I was in 1949, to proclaim that the Communists are our enemies.

I turn now to my own position. I have denied that I am a communist, and I think that in the circumstances I am obliged to state exactly what my political beliefs are.

I have always regarded myself, in the first place, as an African patriot. After all, I was born in Umtata, forty-six years ago. My guardian was my cousin, who was the acting paramount chief of Tembuland, and I am related both to the present paramount chief of Tembuland, Sabata Dalindyebo, and to Kaizer Matanzima, the Chief Minister of the Transkei.

Today I am attracted by the idea of a classless society, an attraction which springs in part from Marxist reading and, in part, from my admiration of the structure and organization of early African societies in this country. The land, then the main means of production, belonged to the tribe. There were no rich or poor and there was no exploitation.

It is true, as I have already stated, that I have been influenced by Marxist thought. But this is also true of many of the leaders of the new independent States. Such widely different persons as Gandhi, Nehru, Nkrumah, and Nasser all acknowledge this fact. We all accept the need for some form of socialism to enable our people to catch up with the advanced countries of this world and to overcome their legacy of extreme poverty. But this does not mean we are Marxists.

Indeed, for my own part, I believe that it is open to debate whether the Communist Party has any specific role to play at this particular stage of our political struggle. The basic task at the present moment is the removal of race discrimination and the attainment of democratic rights on the basis of the Freedom Charter. In so far as that Party furthers this task, I welcome its assistance. I realize that it is one of the means by which people of all races can be drawn into our struggle.

From my reading of Marxist literature and from conversations with Marxists, I have gained the impression that communists regard the parliamentary system of the West as undemocratic and reactionary. But, on the contrary, I am an admirer of such a system.

The Magna Carta, the Petition of Rights, and the Bill of Rights are documents which are held in veneration by democrats throughout the world.

I have great respect for British political institutions, and for the country's system of justice. I regard the British Parliament as the most democratic institution in the world, and the independence and impartiality of its judiciary never fail to arouse my admiration.

The American Congress, that country's doctrine of separation of powers, as well as the independence of its judiciary, arouses in me similar sentiments.

I have been influenced in my thinking by both West and East. All this has led me to feel that in my search for a political formula, I should be absolutely impartial and objective. I should tie myself to no particular system of society other than of socialism. I must leave myself free to borrow the best from the West and from the East . . .

There are certain Exhibits which suggest that we received financial support from abroad, and I wish to deal with this question.

Our political struggle has always been financed from internal sources—from funds raised by our own people and by our own supporters. Whenever we had a special campaign or an important political case—for example, the Treason Trial —we received financial assistance from sympathetic individuals and organizations in the Western countries. We had never felt it necessary to go beyond these sources.

But when in 1961 the Umkhonto was formed, and a new phase of struggle introduced, we realized that these events would make a heavy call on our slender resources, and that the scale of our activities would be hampered by the lack of funds. One of my instructions, as I went abroad in January 1962, was to raise funds from the African states.

I must add that, whilst abroad, I had discussions with leaders of political movements in Africa and discovered that almost every single one of them, in areas which had still not attained independence, had received all forms of assistance from the socialist countries, as well as from the West, including that of financial support. I also discovered that some well-known African states, all of them non-communists, and even anti-communists, had received similar assistance.

On my return to the Republic, I made a strong recommendation to the ANC that we should not confine ourselves to Africa and the Western countries, but that we should also send a mission to the socialist countries to raise the funds which we so urgently needed.

I have been told that after I was convicted such a mission was sent, but I am not prepared to name any countries to which it went, nor am I at liberty to disclose the names of the organizations and countries which gave us support or promised to do so.

As I understand the State case, and in particular the evidence of 'Mr. X', the suggestion is that Umkhonto was the inspiration of the Communist Party which sought by playing upon imaginary grievances to enrol the African people into an army which ostensibly was to fight for African freedom, but in reality was fighting for a communist state. Nothing could be further from the truth. In fact the suggestion is preposterous. Umkhonto was formed by Africans to further their struggle for freedom in their own land. Communists and others supported the movement, and we only wish that more sections of the community would join us.

Our fight is against real, and not imaginary, hardships or, to use the language of the State Prosecutor, 'so-called hardships'. Basically, we fight against two features which are the hallmarks of African life in South Africa and which are entrenched by legislation which we seek to have repealed. These features are poverty and lack of human dignity, and we do not need communists or so-called 'agitators' to teach us about these things.

South Africa is the richest country in Africa, and could be one of the richest countries in the world. But it is a land of extremes and remarkable contrasts. The whites enjoy what may well be the highest standard of living in the world, whilst Africans live in poverty and misery. Forty per cent of the Africans live in hopelessly overcrowded and, in some cases, drought-stricken Reserves, where soil erosion and the overworking of the soil makes it impossible for them to live properly off the land. Thirty per cent are labourers, labour tenants, and squatters on white farms and work and live under conditions similar to those of the serfs of the Middle Ages. The other 30 per cent live in towns where they have developed economic and social habits which bring them closer in many respects to white standards. Yet most Africans, even in this group, are impoverished by low incomes and high cost of living.

The highest-paid and the most prosperous section of urban African life is in Johannesburg. Yet their actual position is desperate. The latest figures were given on 25 March 1964 by Mr. Carr, Manager of the Johannesburg Non-European Affairs Department. The poverty datum line for the average African family in Johannesburg (according to Mr. Carr's department) is R42.84 per month. He showed that the average monthly wage is R32.24 and that 46 per cent of all African families in Johannesburg do not earn enough to keep them going.

Poverty goes hand in hand with malnutrition and disease. The incidence of malnutrition and deficiency diseases is very high amongst Africans. Tuberculosis, pellagra, kwashiorkor, gastro-enteritis, and scurvy bring death and destruction of health. The incidence of infant mortality is one of the highest in the world. According to the Medical Officer of Health for Pretoria, tuberculosis kills forty people a day (almost all Africans), and in 1961 there were 58,491 new cases reported. These diseases not only destroy the vital organs of the body, but they result in retarded mental conditions and lack of initiative, and reduce powers of concentration. The secondary results of such conditions affect the whole community and the standard of work performed by African labourers.

The complaint of Africans, however, is not only that they are poor and the whites are rich, but that the laws which are made by the whites are designed to preserve this situation. There are two ways to break out of poverty. The first is by formal education, and the second is by the worker acquiring a greater skill at his work and thus higher wages. As far as Africans are concerned, both these avenues of advancement are deliberately curtailed by legislation.

The present Government has always sought to hamper Africans in their search for education. One of their early acts, after coming into power, was to stop subsidies for African school feeding. Many African children who attended schools depended on this supplement to their diet. This was a cruel act.

There is compulsory education for all white children at virtually no cost to their parents, be they rich or poor. Similar facilities are not provided for the African children, though there are some who receive such assistance. African children, however, generally have to pay more for their schooling than whites. According to figures quoted by the South African Institute of Race Relations in its 1963 journal, approximately 40 per cent of African children in the age group between seven to fourteen do not attend school. For those who do attend school, the standards are vastly different from those afforded to white children. In 1960-61 the *per capita* Government spending on African students at State-aided schools was estimated at R12.46. In the same years, the *per capita* spending on white children in the Cape Province (which are the only figures available to me) was R144.57. Although there are no figures available to me, it can be stated, without doubt, that the white children on whom R144.57 per head was being spent all came from wealthier homes than African children on whom R12.46 per head was being spent.

The quality of education is also different. According to the Bantu Educational Journal, only 5,660 African children in the whole of South Africa passed their Junior Certificate in 1962, and in that year only 362 passed matric.* This is presumably consistent with the policy of Bantu education about which the present Prime Minister said, during the debate on the Bantu Education Bill in 1953:

"When I have control of Native education I will reform it so that Natives will be taught from childhood to realize that equality with Europeans is not for them . . . People who believe in equality are not desirable teachers for Natives. When my Department controls Native education it will know for what class of higher education a Native is fitted, and whether he will have a chance in life to use his knowledge."

The other main obstacle to the economic advancement of the African is the industrial colour-bar under which all the better jobs of industry are reserved for Whites only. Moreover, Africans who do obtain employment in the unskilled and semi-skilled occupations which are open to them are not allowed to form trade unions which have recognition under the Industrial Conciliation Act. This means that strikes of African workers are illegal, and that they are denied the right of collective bargaining which is permitted to the better-paid White workers. The discrimination in the policy of successive South African Governments towards African workers is demonstrated by the so-called 'civilized labour policy' under which sheltered, unskilled Government jobs are found for those white workers who cannot make the grade in industry, at wages which far exceed the earnings of the average African employee in industry.

The Government often answers its critics by saying that Africans in South Africa are economically better off than the inhabitants of the other countries in Africa. I do not know whether this statement is true and doubt whether any comparison can be made without having regard to the cost-of-living index in such countries. But even if it is true, as far as the African people are concerned it is irrelevant. Our complaint is not that we are poor by comparison with people in other countries, but that we are poor by comparison with the white people in our own country, and that we are prevented by legislation from altering this imbalance.

---

*The Junior Certificate examination was generally taken by white children at the age of 15 and they cannot normally leave school before this. Matriculation is taken two years later and qualifies students for higher education. The educational system, however, ensures that very few Africans reach Junior Certificate level, so that what represents a basic standard for whites is one of achievement for Africans. Even fewer attain matriculation level.

The lack of human dignity experienced by Africans is the direct result of the policy of white supremacy. White supremacy implies black inferiority. Legislation designed to preserve white supremacy entrenches this notion. Menial tasks in South Africa are invariably performed by Africans. When anything has to be carried or cleaned the white man will look around for an African to do it for him, whether the African is employed by him or not. Because of this sort of attitude, whites tend to regard Africans as a separate breed. They do not look upon them as people with families of their own; they do not realize that they have emotions—that they fall in love like white people do; that they want to be with their wives and children like white people want to be with theirs; that they want to earn enough money to support their families properly, to feed and clothe them and send them to school. And what 'house-boy' or 'garden-boy' or labourer can ever hope to do this?

Pass laws, which to the Africans are among the most hated bits of legislation in South Africa, render any African liable to police surveillance at any time. I doubt whether there is a single African male in South Africa who has not at some stage had a brush with the police over his pass. Hundreds and thousands of Africans are thrown into jail each year under pass laws. Even worse than this is the fact that pass laws keep husband and wife apart and lead to the breakdown of family life.

Poverty and the breakdown of family life have secondary effects. Children wander about the streets of the townships because they have no schools to go to, or no money to enable them to go to school, or no parents at home to see that they go to school, because both parents (if there be two) have to work to keep the family alive. This leads to a breakdown in moral standards, to an alarming rise in illegitimacy, and to growing violence which erupts not only politically, but everywhere. Life in the townships is dangerous. There is not a day that goes by without somebody being stabbed or assaulted. And violence is carried out of the townships in the white living areas. People are afraid to walk alone in the streets after dark. Housebreakings and robberies are increasing, despite the fact that the death sentence can now be imposed for such offences. Death sentences cannot cure the festering sore.

Africans want to be paid a living wage. Africans want to perform work which they are capable of doing, and not work which the Government declares them to be capable of. Africans want to be allowed to live where they obtain work, and not be endorsed out of an area because they were not born there. Africans want to be allowed to own land in places where they work, and not to be obliged to live in rented houses which they can never call their own. Africans want to be part of the general population, and not confined to living in their own ghettoes. African men want to have their wives and children to live with them where they work, and not be forced into an unnatural existence in men's hostels. African women want to be with their menfolk and not be left permanently widowed in the Reserves. Africans want to be allowed out after eleven o'clock at night and not to be confined to their rooms like little children. Africans want to be allowed to travel in their own country and to seek work where they want to and not where the Labour Bureau tells them to. Africans want a just share in the whole of South Africa; they want security and a stake in society.

Above all, we want equal political rights, because without them our disabilities will be permanent. I know this sounds revolutionary to the whites in this country, because the majority of voters will be Africans. This makes the white man fear democracy.

But this fear cannot be allowed to stand in the way of the only solution which will guarantee racial harmony and freedom for all. It is not true that the enfranchisement of all will result in racial domination. Political division, based on colour, is entirely artificial and, when it disappears, so will the domination of one colour group by another. The ANC has spent half a century fighting against racialism. When it triumphs it will not change that policy.

This then is what the ANC is fighting. Their struggle is a truly national one. It is a struggle of the African people, inspired by their own suffering and their own experience. It is a struggle for the right to live.

During my lifetime I have dedicated myself to this struggle of the African people. I have fought against white domination, and I have fought against black domination. I have cherished the ideal of a democratic and free society in which all persons live together in harmony and with equal opportunities. It is an ideal which I hope to live for and to achieve. But if needs be, it is an ideal for which I am prepared to die.

On 11 June 1964, at the conclusion of the trial, Mandela and seven others— Walter Sisulu, Govan Mbeki, Raymond Mhlaba, Elias Motsoaledi, Andrew Mlangeni, Ahmed Kathrada and Denis Goldberg— were convicted. Mandela was found guilty on four charges of sabotage and like the others was sentenced to life imprisonment.

Latest Publications
from IDAF

WALVIS BAY — Namibia's Port
by Richard Moorsom. Published 1984.
96 pp., illustrated **Price £1.50.**

Reviews both the history and the future consequences of continued South African control of Walvis Bay; the importance of the harbour and its fishing industry; and the build-up of South African military strength in the area.

CLASS & COLOUR in South Africa 1850-1950
by Jack and Ray Simons. Reprinted 1983.
702 pp. **Price £5.00.**

"Few books published on South Africa can have built up quite such a reputation as this history, first printed in 1969 ... enormously informative ... IDAF is to be congratulated not only on taking this initiative but in also keeping the price down." — LABOUR WEEKLY.

APARTHEID THE FACTS
by IDAF Research, Information and Publications Dept.
Published 1983. 112 pp., illustrated **Price £3.00.**

". . . with facts, figures, photographs, maps and graphs . . . suitable for a first time reader, it will also provide useful background and analysis for those with some previous knowledge." — LABOUR RESEARCH.

NAMIBIA — THE RAVAGES OF WAR
by Barbara König. Published 1983.
60 pp., illustrated **Price £1.50.**

". . . Lays bare the system of oppression and its dire consequences . . . thoroughly informative." — CARIBBEAN TIMES.

AKIN TO SLAVERY — Prison Labour in South Africa
by Allen Cook. Published 1982.
81 pp. **Price 50p.**

"Reveals the extent to which the prison labour system, far from disappearing, remains an integral part of Apartheid." — ONE WORLD.

All these books can be obtained direct from International Defence and Aid Fund for Southern Africa, Canon Collins House, 64 Essex Rd., London N1 8LR. A full list of publications is available on request.

Printed by A. G. Bishop & Sons Ltd., Orpington, Kent.